VIRGINIA:

The English Heritage in America

"I dream of a new English nation in Virginia."

SIR WALTER RALEIGH

VIRGINIA:

The English Heritage in America

The story in text and pictures of England's first permanent colony in the New World, from its founding in 1607 through the years of its leadership to American nationhood.

By Parke Rouse, Jr.

HASTINGS HOUSE *Publishers*   New York

For my Mother

Pauline Dashiell Rouse

OBVERSE

THE GREAT SEAL

REVERSE

Contents

Acknowledgments

My desire to write this account of Virginia's early years grew out of my work in preparation for the Jamestown Festival of 1957, which celebrated the 350th anniversary of Virginia's settlement. Much of what is presented here results from research which I undertook as Executive Director of the Virginia 350th Anniversary Commission and, since 1958, of The Jamestown Foundation of the Commonwealth of Virginia.

I am indebted to the Honorable Lewis A. McMurran Jr., chairman of those commissions, for his encouragement. Also helpful have been Mr. Harold Midgley, O.B.E., director of the photographs division of the Central Office of Information of the British government, and Mr. Samuel M. Bemiss, chairman of the Jamestown Committee of the Association for the Preservation of Virginia Antiquities. From the National Park Service, which shares with the APVA the administration of Jamestown, I have enjoyed the cordial assistance of Mr. Charles E. Hatch, chief park historian of Colonial National Historical Park, and of Mr. Paul Hudson, museum curator of that park.

Tremendous assistance was rendered by Dr. Richard L. Morton, chairman emeritus of the department of history at the College of William and Mary, whose two-volume *Colonial Virginia* is the definitive history of Virginia until 1763. I also owe gratitude to Dr. James Servies, librarian of the college; Dr. Thaddeus Tate, associate professor of history; and Mr. Herbert Ganter, archivist of the college. Members of the Research Department of Colonial Williamsburg who have been of assistance include Dr. Edward M. Riley, director; Mrs. Mary Mordecai Goodwin, Miss Mary Stephenson, and Mrs. Rose Belk. My especial thanks go to Mr. Jack Morpurgo, director of the National Book League, of London, who made many helpful suggestions.

Among my colleagues on the staff of the Jamestown Foundation, I wish to thank Mr. Pembroke Thomas, curator, and Mrs. Elizabeth Emmerson, Mrs. Margaret Grey, Mrs. Erica Benjamin, and Miss Hansford Patteson. For advice on Virginia's military history, I thank General Edwin Cox; Mr. Harold Peterson, chief curator of the U. S. Department of the Interior; and Mr. Wilcomb Washburn, curator of the Division of Political History of the Smithsonian Institution. Thanks are also expressed to Mrs. Jacqueline Chapman for her research.

For useful genealogical information I am indebted to Mrs. Annie Lash Jester, who compiled with the late Mrs. Martha Woodroof Hiden the useful *Adventurers of Purse and Person* for publication by the Order of First Families of Virginia in 1957. I salute Commander Walter Raleigh Gilbert of Paignton, England, for information on his forebears, Sir Humphrey Gilbert and Sir Walter Raleigh.

In assembling illustrations I have depended chiefly on resources of the Virginia State Library, the Valentine Museum of Richmond, and Colonial Williamsburg. I am particularly indebted to Mrs. Katherine M. Smith of the library; Miss Elizabeth Dance of the museum; and Mrs. Eileen Newman and Mrs. Jean Sheldon of Colonial Williamsburg. Photographs have kindly been provided by Mr. Hugh DeSamper and Miss Marguerite Gignilliat of Colonial Williamsburg and by Mr. Philip Flournoy of the Virginia State Chamber of Commerce.

The pictures used are credited individually, but I would like to express special thanks to Mr. Aubrey Bodine for permitting use of his photograph of the three reconstructed Jamestown ships at Jamestown Festival Park; to Mr. Thomas L. Williams, who copied many photographs used herein; and to Mr. William Gravitt for preparing two maps. Appreciation is expressed to Mr. Russell Bourne of American Heritage Publishing Company for permission to use three illustrations from its useful juvenile publication, *Jamestown:*

First English Colony, and to Harcourt, Brace & World, Inc., for permission to use a quotation from Vernon Louis Parrington's *The Romantic Revolution in America*, in the Epilogue. I wish to thank Mrs. Robert Kincaid for permission to reproduce the map of the Wilderness Road from the book of that title by her late husband. Mr. Leslie Cheek, director of the Virginia Museum of Fine Arts, and Mr. Charles Montgomery, librarian, have also been most cooperative.

I record here my appreciation of the work of three scholars of past years which has benefitted me as it has many others: the late Mrs. Martha Woodroof Hiden, who preserved many valuable records and who wrote knowingly of early Virginia; the late Dr. Earl G. Swem, librarian of the College of William and Mary and editor of the useful Virginia historical index; and the late Alexander Wilbourne Weddell, whose *Historical Virginia Portraiture* remains a fascinating book years after its publication.

Lastly and chiefly, I express my gratitude to my secretary, Mrs. Veronica Payne, for her patience in preparing the manuscript for publication; and to my wife, whose encouragement has kept me plugging away despite interruptions and delays. Without her it would have been impossible.

PARKE ROUSE, JR.

Foreword

The east coast of North America was English for 175 years before it became American. The English first explored it in 1497, claimed it in 1584, and proudly named it Virginia for their virgin queen, Elizabeth. It was the beginning of their empire overseas, and their maps showed it as a vast domain bounded by the Atlantic on the east, an unknown sea on the west, and an uninhabited land which they called Norumbega to the north, whence English trawlers ventured each spring in search of codfish.

To the south, Virginia's line was cautiously drawn above the Gulf of Mexico to avert complaint from Spain, which had settled St. Augustine in 1565 and which claimed the romantic land which Juan Ponce de Leon had named Pascua Florida (Feast of Flowers) in 1512.

After many unsuccessful efforts, the English finally planted themselves firmly in Virginia in 1607. So successful was the Virginia territory in attracting English settlers that by the American Revolution it had been divided into 13 English colonies. Of these, the original Virginia colony was always the largest and most populous by far.

Foreword   [13]

Because her charter had given her the lion's share of unexplored lands west of the Atlantic coastal settlements, Virginia steadily pushed her frontier westward for 175 years to the Mississippi River and the Great Lakes against the will of native Indians, of the French, and finally — in 1774 — against redcoats from the English motherland itself, after Britain attempted to wrest the Northwest from Virginia and make it a province of Canada. However, Virginia troops under George Rogers Clark held it fast.

It was England's hope from the beginning to span the continent and control the inland sea — the Great Lakes — which ancient mariners believed to lead westward from Virginia to the shadowy Pacific. That ambitious plan was Virginia policy from Captain Christopher Newport's exploration of the James River in 1607 through the years when young George Washington fought the French and Indians in the Ohio Territory. It convinced President Jefferson that acquisition of the Louisiana Territory from France was the nation's destiny, and it gave him opportunity to indulge his boundless curiosity by sending Meriwether Lewis and William Clark west in 1805 to find the longed-for water route to the Pacific.

The same continent-consciousness also led James Monroe in 1823 to shut the door to further European colonization in the United States' sphere, and it hastened the union's acceptance of the Texas territory in 1845, in the administration of President John Tyler, also a Virginian.

After the colonies became states of the union in 1788, Virginia gave up her western lands to create new states. In this process, the Virginia territory which had once been almost a nation in itself was reduced to a size not much larger than its neighbors. Still, the romance and great deeds of her early years stuck in the consciousness of the nation.

In exploring and settling much of North America, Virginia's people helped permanently to implant there the English language, law, and a system of individual enterprise which gave to every man — except in the years of slavery's blight — opportunities which have built a great nation. Even after later waves of immigration swept in from Ireland, Germany, Scandinavia, and other nations, America's inheritance remains dominantly English. The most important fact of the modern world, mused Bismarck sadly before his death, is that Great Britain and the United States speak the same tongue.

In this historic development, which strongly affects our twentieth century world, early Virginia played a major role. I have tried to tell it here.

PARKE ROUSE, JR.

Jamestown, Virginia

List of Illustrations

The Jamestown Church
The Christopher Wren Building
The Capitol at Williamsburg

Washington and Lee University
Mount Vernon
Cumberland Gap

1 Spain Claims the New World

SPAIN'S AMBITIONS CHALLENGE ENGLAND: *After the New World is discovered in 1492, Spain and Portugal plant settlements there. Great Britain, a growing power, challenges their claims in 1585. Raleigh names part of North America Virginia to honor the Virgin Queen, Elizabeth.*

1

Spain Claims the New World

Early in the morning of October 12, 1492, a lookout aboard Columbus' ship *Pinta* first spied San Salvador, in the West Indies. Thus was the modern world glimpsed. From that moment on, man's horizon doubled. Not one hemisphere but two were now his world, greatly extending the orbit of his interests and his ambitions.'

The initiative in this extension belonged without doubt to Spain. Christopher Columbus, although a Genoan, had sailed under the flag and patronage of King Ferdinand and Queen Isabella of Spain. In exploration as in conquest, the prize goes to the first claimant. Clearly the New World had been discovered by Spain. Although Portuguese

had led Europe's exploration earlier in the century, their efforts had lagged since the death of Prince Henry the Navigator, in 1460. While Portugal was seeking a sea route around Africa to the East which would break the monopoly which Venice held on the spice trade, Columbus in one great sweep opened up a hemisphere.

To confirm Spain's claim, Pope Alexander VI in the year after Columbus' voyage granted to Spain's King Ferdinand II the new discoveries west and south of India. But Portugal objected, and in 1494 the division of the World's lands between the two leading seafaring powers was revised and proclaimed in a treaty signed at Tordesillas,

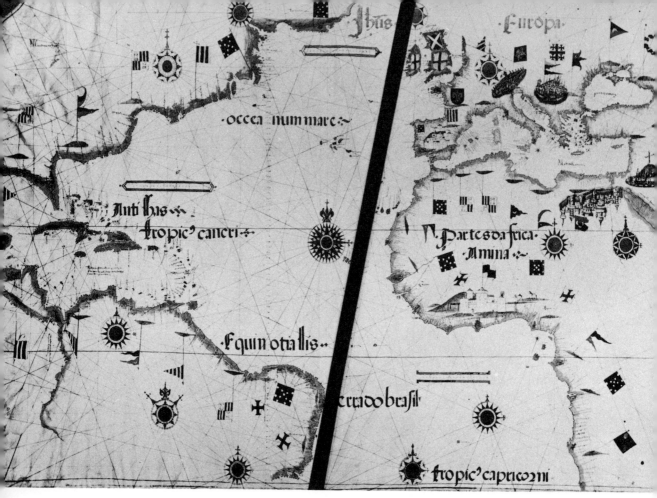

Pope Alexander VI in 1493 divided the New World between the Roman Catholic rulers of Spain and Portugal. Spain was authorized to settle in the territory left of the line and Portugal in the lands to the west. *Thomas L. Williams from The Jamestown Foundation*

Spain, by King Ferdinand and by King John II of Portugal. It was agreed that Spain would enjoy all rights of trade and settlement in new lands west of a line of demarcation 370 leagues west of the Cape Verde Islands, while smaller Portugal would possess the lands east of that line.

The practical effect of this division was to give Spain all territory except the part of South America which Portugal was to settle as Brazil.

Most of Europe's nations were too weak or too deeply involved in other problems in 1494 to contest the claims of Spain and Portugal. France, which vied with Spain as the leading continental power, was exhausted by her Hundred Years' War with England and by her loss to Spain of the Italian wars. The sea-girt Scandinavian kingdoms were then united, but their ambitions were limited by their size. Italy dominated the intellectual and artistic life of Europe through the wonders of her Renaissance, but politically her divided city states were victimized by the nations around them. The Netherlands was a ferment of rival powers. Russia, remote and inscrutable, was just beginning to bend the power of her nobles to her king.

One small island nation on the northern fringe of Europe refused to accept Spanish domination of the New World. England was developing a navy and a desire for empire, and she resented the Pope's disposition of the new lands. Accordingly, two years after Spain and Portugal had signed the Treaty of Tordesillas, King Henry VII licensed John Cabot or Cabotto, a Venetian living in Bristol, to sail in search of a sea route to the East. Spanish agents in London protested, but Cabot made two voyages which were to establish England's claims for the first time to New World lands.

Embarking in 1497 and in 1498, he made the first two voyages across the North Atlantic since the Vikings, and he discovered and explored Newfoundland, Nova Scotia, and the North American coast as far south, evidently, as Chesapeake Bay. The royal standard of England's king, which Cabot planted at Cape Breton, Newfoundland, was to be the basis for England's claims in the New World for the next 90 years.

Cabot's discoveries worried the Spanish. A map drawn by the Biscayan pilot Juan de la Cosa in 1500 reflects information that Cabot had gathered and shows the North American coastline dotted with the flag of England's King. To prevent further English claims, the King and Queen of Spain in 1501 commissioned Alonso de Hojeda to follow the Venezuelan coastline, "setting up marks with the arms of their Majesties" that all who came might see.

England's steady growth as a sea power began with Cabot's voyages and continued slowly for a century while Spain laid claims to new lands through the explorations of Juan Ponce de Leon, Ferdinand Magellan, and Vasco Nunez de Balboa; and while Portugal reaped the discoveries of Vasco da Gama, Pedro Alvarez Cabral, and many others. On the heels of Spanish exploration, Diego de Velazquez settled Cuba in 1511. Ponce de Leon, discovering Florida in 1512, gave Spain opportunity to create a supply base for its Caribbean trade in 1565. In 1521 the Spanish king imposed his ruthless rule on Mexico with Hernando Cortes' capture of Mexico City, and in 1535 he strengthened his grasp on South America with Pizarro's conquest of Peru.

Clearly the sixteenth century was proving a triumph for Spanish and Portuguese settlement, with Spain dominant in the New World and Portugal in the Near East, the Indies, and China.

England chafed under the limitations of a second-rate power and yearned for the day when she could challenge Spain as equal. To hasten this day, King Henry VII gave England her first navy. His son, the powerful Henry VIII, built larger and deadlier ships and defied the Roman Catholic world of Spain and Portugal by refusing to concede to the Pope supremacy over England's sovereign and her church.

The rapid growth of home industry and of towns in sixteenth century England was turning the island into a nation of shopkeepers, ambitious and independent of mind, and it spurred the building of merchant ships in an effort to break the control which the Mediterranean powers had exercised over European commerce since before the Middle Ages. Clearly, England in the decades which followed Columbus' discovery was a nation determined to wield power outside its narrow boundaries.

When Queen Elizabeth ascended the throne in 1558, the English sensed that the time for their challenge had come. Elizabeth was the spirited daughter of King Henry

Imperious Queen Elizabeth spurred England's captains to explore and claim land in the New World. *Colonial Williamsburg*

VIII, and she shared her father's thirst for power. Like him, she was a master manipulator of men, and she had the added advantage of being a woman whose elusive favors were sought by kings, courtiers, and captains alike. In her long reign she harnessed the spiritual and physical energies of her people and directed them to the expansion of England's glory.

"Make them earn their honor," she barked of her courtiers, "and by pain and peril purchase what piece of credit or profit is bestowed on them."

From the hour of her enthronement until her death 45 years later, Elizabeth inspired the exploits of a succession of sea captains and explorers who advanced England on land and sea. Taking advantage of the temporary peace with Spain which followed Elizabeth's accession, Sir John Hawkins embarked on the first of three slave-taking expeditions to the Spanish possessions in the Caribbean area.

In 1577 Sir Francis Drake became the first Englishman to circle the globe, repeating Magellan's exploit for Spain 55 years before. During this voyage the daring Drake landed on the California coast, in or near the present San Francisco Bay, seeking to chart the other shore of the unknown North American land mass that John Cabot had reached 80 years earlier by way of the North Atlantic. In the same period Sir Martin Frobisher was exploring the Labrador coast, probing for a northwest passage to the Pacific, and John Davis was discovering the strait later named for him between Greenland and Baffin Bay, connecting the Atlantic and the Baffin Sea. These were but a few of the explorations which took place in Elizabeth's reign.

English businessmen backed such efforts in hopes of trade with newly-opened regions. The pattern was cut with the chartering in 1556 of the Muscovy Company for trade with the East by way of Russia. Sebastian Cabot, son of John, was a leader in this enterprise, which was quaintly titled "The Mystery and Company of the Merchant Adventurers for the Discovery of Regions, Dominions, Islands, and Places Unknown." In 1581 the Levant Company was chartered by Elizabeth, and two years later

Sir John Hawkins Knight

His shadow to the world brave Hawkins shewes,
Who was a Bulwark to his friends, to foes
Royalles Thunder; who for countries sake
So many a hard attempt durst vndertake
The Indian in their barbarous tongues do praise him,
And vnto Heauen his very foes doe raise him,
He in his life whole Seas could bound y time.
Let not then feeble Rymer drowne his name. SH.

Sir John Hawkins commanded slave-taking voyages against Spanish colonies in America early in Elizabeth's reign. RIGHT: Sir Francis Drake, in 1577 the first Englishman to circle the globe. *National Maritime Museum, Greenwich, England*

it placed its first agent in Constantinople. In 1583 came the Venice Company, and in 1600 the East India Company.

In each case, shares in the enterprise were bought by individuals and companies, yielding the capital to buy or rent ships. All these ventures were private enterprises, created primarily for profit rather than for national growth or the planting of colonies.

But there were some Englishmen who saw the advantage of government-sponsored colonization, and chief among them were Sir Humphrey Gilbert and his half brother, Sir Walter Raleigh. In his *Discourse to prove a Passage by the North West to Cathaia*, which he presented to the Queen in 1574, Gilbert and his silent collaborator, Raleigh, argued the value of permanent overseas settlements and asked permission to plant them. The Queen agreed, and Sir Humphrey made two voyages in behalf of his project before being lost at sea on a homeward trip from Newfoundland in 1583. As his tiny ten-ton ship, the *Squirrel*, went down in a raging storm, Sir Humphrey was heard by the crew aboard

Spain Claims the New World   [27]

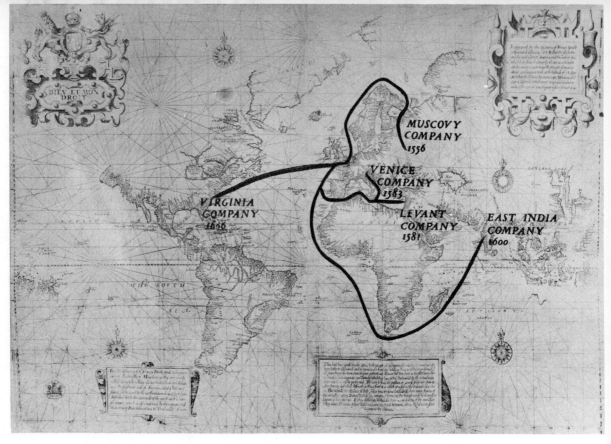

England's overseas trade was promoted by a series of privately-supported ventures that began with the chartering of the Muscovy Company in 1555 by Sebastian Cabot. Then came the Levant Company in 1581, Venice in 1583, East India in 1600, and the chartering of the Virginia Company in 1606. *The Jamestown Foundation*

the consort vessel gallantly consoling his men, "We are as near to heaven by sea as by land."

Good will between Spain and England did not last long after Elizabeth's enthronement. The Queen's Protestant beliefs and nationalistic policies jarred his Catholic majesty, King Philip II of Spain, and she relentlessly pressed England's challenge. The boldest stroke came in 1585, when Sir Francis Drake led a fleet of 23 vessels from England across the Atlantic to attack Spanish holdings in the New World. The object was to take Havana, in Cuba, and Cartagena, in Colombia, and thus cut off Spain's transatlantic trade, which supported her war in Europe. The operation partly succeeded. Drake looted Santo Domingo and Cartagena, but Havana proved too strong to attack. Spain could not be dislodged.

During these years the pressure for overseas colonization which Gilbert had originated was renewed by Sir Walter Raleigh. He once had been a favorite of Queen Elizabeth — some said a lover — until he had compromised her lady-in-waiting, Elizabeth Throckmorton, and married her. He was still a man of influence and following in the lusty world of Elizabethan London. As poet he was often in the company of Shakespeare and that galaxy of Elizabethan writers whose fame shines through the ages. As courtier, he knew the powerful men of Court, Parliament, and the city of London. All his life he had hoped to colonize the New World and, as he put it, to plant "a new English nation in Virginia." From the time of his boyhood on the Devon coast of England, he had gazed at the Atlantic's horizon and dreamed of what lay beyond. He was motivated both by the mystical religious impulse of a Crusader and by hopes of knightly glory, for Raleigh was both spirit-

ual and worldly, like many of his fellow Elizabethans.

In 1584 Raleigh received from the Queen a hard-sought patent similar to Gilbert's, authorizing him to plant the long-awaited English settlement on the North American coast. It empowered him "to discover and to plant Christian inhabitants in places convenient upon those large and ample countries extended northward from the cape of Florida, not in the actual possession of any

English mariners believed North America to be a narrow continent, bounded on the west by the Sea of China and the Indies. Sir Francis Drake landed on the present California shore in 1577 and claimed the San Francisco Bay area in the name of Queen Elizabeth. *National Park Service*

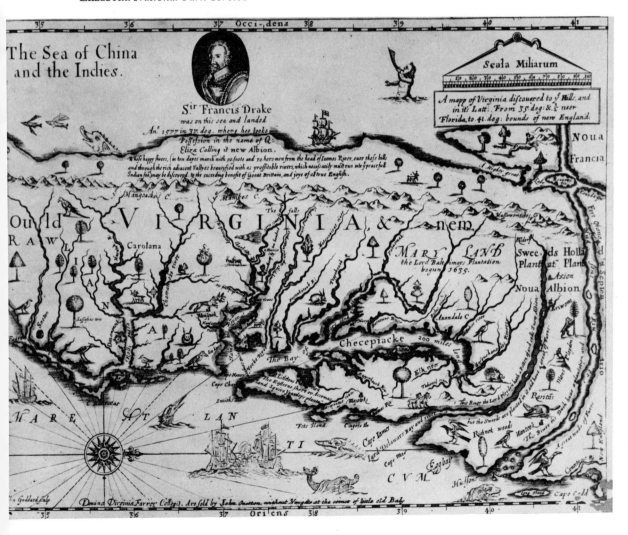

Sebastian Cabot accompanied his father John Cabot on his voyages to North America in 1497 and 1498 and helped form the Muscovy Company to promote English trade with Russia. *British Official Photograph*

with the garb and beatific mien of the Virgin Mary, and poets apostrophized her as England's savior. She was celebrated as the queen

> *Who sent her navies hence*
> *Unto the either Inde*
>   *and to that shore so green*
> *Virginia, which we call of her,*
> *A virgin queen.*

The three voyages which Raleigh undertook, beginning in 1584, were the first systematic attempt by the English to study and to colonize North America. The first was to explore the land lying behind the Outer Banks of the present North Carolina, a chain of islands stretching from Cape Lookout northward almost to the Virginia Capes. The second effort, in the year 1585-86, was the colonization of a hundred-odd persons under the leadership of Sir Richard Grenville at Roanoke Island, in the same area. The third desperate venture, in 1587, was intended to renew the colony, but to the bewilderment of the rescuers and of posterity, hardly a trace of the settlers could be found except for a single word, CROATOAN, carved on a tree.

In the failure of this well-planned and relatively well-financed effort, Sir Walter Raleigh lost his chance to be the founder of English civilization in the New World. Losing also what remained of the Queen's favor, he never again attempted to plant a colony in Virginia and at last was imprisoned in the Tower of London by Elizabeth's successor, King James I. There he learned in 1606 of the embarkation of more would-be settlers for Virginia, sailing from a dock in London close to his cell in the Tower, and there he died at the gallows in

Christian prince." The patent defined the claim as the unexplored lands between latitudes 34° and 45° North, which extends northward from the present Cape Fear, in North Carolina, to the upper boundary of Maine.

To England's claim Raleigh gave the name Virginea or Virginia, in honor of Her Virgin Majesty. The choice of the name was an inspired one, for England's admiration for her Queen extended almost to worship, especially after her victory over King Philip II. Paintings and statues depicted her

VERA EFFIGIES CLARISS.ⁱ VIRI DOM̃ⁱⁿ GUALTHERI RALEGH EQV. AUR. &c.

The true and lively portraiture of the honourable and learned Knight Sʳ Walter Ralegh.

AMORE ET VIRTVTE

HVMFRIDVS GILBERTVS MILES AVRATVS &c.

Quid Non

GILBERTVS ciues alium deduxit in orbem. Quò CHRISTI imbuerit barbara colla fide. AB

Sir Walter Raleigh and his half-brother, Sir Humphrey Gilbert, urged that England settle colonists overseas to strengthen and enrich her. *National Park Service*
RIGHT: Sir Humphrey Gilbert was the first Englishman to attempt to settle a colony in North America. He was lost at sea in 1583. *National Maritime Museum, Greenwich*

1618, a victim of his ambitions for England.

In Raleigh's failure in Virginia, England almost lost her opportunity to grasp the green continent whereon Cabot had planted the English royal standard nearly a hundred years earlier. It could have been a fatal blow to her global ambitions. Had not Elizabeth's navy and a ragged array of merchantmen defeated King Philip's Spanish Armada so decisively in 1588 and prevented an invasion of England, his dream of "a new English nation" could not have been realized. As it turned out, the triumph of British sea-power was so overwhelming that Spain was never again to be the colossus of the seas.

No longer was England a second-class power. After 1588, the New World lay waiting for her.

Unable to capture England and out-sailed and outfought by Drake, Hawkins, and Elizabeth's other captains, Spain at last signed a treaty of peace with England in 1604. England agreed to respect Spanish claims to all territory that Spain occupied,

Sir Humphrey Gilbert lands in Newfoundland. *The Mansell Collection, London*

In his boyhood on the Devon coast Walter Raleigh heard tales of distant lands that spurred his desire to explore and settle the New World. *Painting by Sir John Millais, Tate Gallery, London*

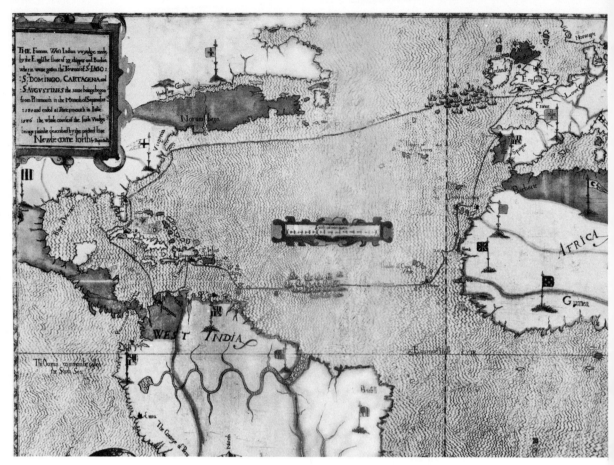

Drake's bold transatlantic crossing in 1585 to attack Spanish holdings. A contemporary map is titled: "The famous West Indian voyage made by the Englishe fleetes of 23 shippes and barkes wherein weare gotten the townes of St. Iago, Sto. Domingo, Cartagena, and St. Augustine, the same beinge begonne from Plymouth in the month of September, 1585, and ended at Portsmouth in Iulie, 1586 . . ."

but the English recognized no Spanish rights in the unoccupied lands of America. The nation-to-be that Queen Elizabeth had defined and Raleigh had named was theirs by right, they felt. All that remained was to settle it. Why did England delay?

In his heroic "Ode to the Virginian Voyage," the English poet Michael Drayton in 1606 dared his countrymen to fulfill their destiny in the New World:

You brave heroic minds,
Worthy your country's name,
That honor still pursue,
Go and subdue,
Whilst loitering hinds
Lurk here at home with shame. . . .

Then Drayton held out the prospect of gain, which sometimes moves men when patriotism fails:

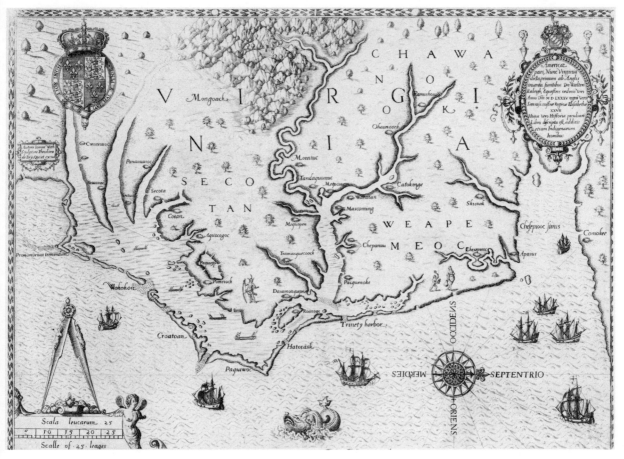

A part of the Virginia coast now the Outer Banks of North Carolina was portrayed by John White, who was sent out by Raleigh in his attempted settlements in 1585 and 1588. In the foreground is Cape Hatteras. *From Theodor de Bry's "The True Pictures and Fashions of the People in That Part of America Now Called Virginia, Discovered by Englishmen . . ."*

And cheerfully at sea
Success you still entice
 To get the pearl and gold
 And ours to hold
Vir-gi-ni-a
Earth's only paradise! . . .

Virginia had not long to wait.

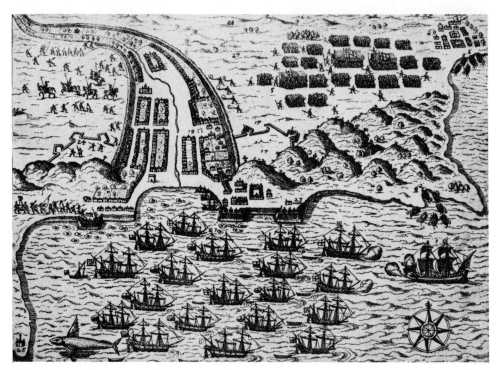

On January 1, 1586, Drake's English fleet captured Santo Domingo. When a British envoy was murdered by the Spanish, Drake hanged two Spanish friars. *National Maritime Museum, Greenwich*

The victory of Queen Elizabeth's navy and merchantmen over the Spanish Armada in 1588 prevented an invasion of England. It also opened the seas to England. *From "Franciscus Dracus Redivivus"*

2   The English Challenge Spain's Claim

THE BEGINNING OF GOVERNMENT BY LAW: *In 1606 English investors organize The Virginia Company to claim and settle Virginia. In 1607 the colony is established at Jamestown and survives despite adversities. John Rolfe acquires Spanish tobacco seed from West Indies and South America and establishes a trade that nurtures Virginia through the next two centuries. In 1619 government by law replaces military authority at Jamestown.*

2

The English Challenge Spain's Claim

Elizabeth did not live to see England's standard planted in the New World, but the event did not long follow her death. When the great Queen died at Richmond Palace in 1603 and King James VI of Scotland was called to London to become James I of England, other Virginia ventures were already under way. Raleigh sent out one last forlorn expedition in 1602 under Samuel Mace, who "performed nothing, but returned with idle stories and frivolous allegations." In the next two years three other English expeditions explored parts of Virginia, one under Bartholomew Gosnold, one under Martin Pring, and a third under Bartholomew Gilbert, son of the ill-fated Sir

Humphrey. None contributed greatly to the sum of England's knowledge.

A more colorful voyage was made by George Weymouth in 1605 to North Virginia, as the New England area was called, bringing back five Indians to excite the interest of London's masses in the New World. A popular comedy, *Eastward Ho*, produced in London in 1605 with interpolations by Ben Jonson, also spread what was called "the Virginia fever."

Audiences gasped at Captain Seagull's description of Virginia to his two companions in a London tavern scene:

"I tell thee, gold is more plentiful there than copper is with us; and for as much red copper as I can bring, I'll have thrice the weight in gold. Why, man, all their dripping-pans . . . are pure gold; and all the chains with which they chain up their streets are massy gold. All the prisoners they take are fettered in gold; and for rubies and diamonds they go forth on holidays and gather 'em by the seashore to hang on their children's coats, and stick in their children's caps, as commonly as our children wear saffron-gilt brooches and groats with holes in 'em."

Four editions of this hit play were published in four months. They greatly stimulated interest in overseas settlement, as well they might!

In 1606 King James I granted to a group of London investors the charter under which England's first permanent settlement was to be established. The Virginia Company of London was headed by Sir Thomas Smythe, the leading London businessman of his day, and its stock was variously bought by wealthy nobles, by merchants, and by London's powerful city companies, which had evolved from trade guilds in the Middle Ages into fraternal bodies with philanthropic and promotional aims. For a subscription of 12 pounds and 10 shillings — about $900 by today's standards — the company offered to make the investor "lord of 200 acres of land," to be issued "to him and his heirs forever."

The company leased from the Muscovy Company two small merchant vessels recently engaged in coal shipment from the British Isles to Russia, and it engaged Christopher Newport, who had crossed the Atlantic nearly a dozen times, and Bartholomew Gosnold, also a veteran sailor, as two of its captains. A call was sent out for men to make the voyage and to remain in Virginia as colonists.

King James VI of Scotland became King James I of England in 1603 on the death of Queen Elizabeth. He continued to promote exploration and settlement. *Association for the Preservation of Virginia Antiquities*

The charter of the company defined the limits of Virginia's coast in the same terms as Queen Elizabeth's to Raleigh twenty-two years before, with the hope of avoiding conflict with "other Christian princes." The Spanish remained in Florida, and a French settlement had just been made, in 1605, to the north at Acadia, or Nova Scotia. The western limit of Virginia was defined as 100 miles inland of the seacoast, which was amended in a second charter in 1609 to read "from sea to sea."

Despite the findings of Hernando De Soto and Francisco Coronado, of Spain, that a continuous land mass stretched from Florida to California, King James and his advisers believed a tributary of Chesapeake Bay could be found that would lead through a narrow land mass to "the South Sea," or

Pacific. Full realization of North America's vast extent did not reach England for a hundred years after Virginia had been settled.

The sector of Virginia assigned by King James for settlement by the Virginia Company of London extended from the 34th to the 41st parallels, or from the present South Carolina to Massachusetts. To a second joint stock company, organized by Plymouth business interests and designated the Virginia Company of Plymouth, the crown assigned lands between the 38th and 45th parallels. The overlap of the two companies' interest between the 38th and 41st parallels was a shrewd device of the King's to develop competition between the companies

Sir Thomas Smythe, leading London businessman, headed the Virginia Company, which in 1606 dispatched 105 colonists to settle in Virginia. *The Jamestown Foundation*

and hasten settlement. The ultimate effect was to divide the Virginia territory into three rather than two zones. The three zones roughly correspond today to the Upper South, the Central Atlantic States, and New England.

The expedition led by Christopher Newport sailed from Blackwall docks on the Thames on December 20, 1606, in order to complete the anticipated four-month voyage and reach Virginia in time for spring planting. In a lengthy directive to the voyagers, His Majesty's Council for Virginia prescribed that Newport should have "sole charge and command of all captains, soldiers, mariners, and other persons that shall go." From several dozen English voyages to North America since John Cabot's, Newport and Gosnold knew the outward passage would be safest by the long South Atlantic route. Accordingly, the holds of the 100-ton *Susan Constant*, the 40-ton *Godspeed*, and the 20-ton *Discovery* were crammed with food, ale, and wine, together with seed oats, barley, and wheat; cumbersome matchlock muskets, gunpowder, metal breastplates, and helmets for protection. Also on board were altar vessels, bibles, and prayer books for their spiritual comfort; beads and baubles for barter with the Indians; building tools and farm implements; and dozens of other articles needed to build homes in the wilderness, thousands of miles from England.

The heavy helmets and breastplates were relics of medieval combat, no longer needed in Europe since the advent of gunpowder and the ponderous matchlock gun. However, earlier explorers had found them effective against Indian arrows. Accordingly, they were loaded aboard ship at Blackwall docks.

Atop their tall masts the ships flew the new union flag, adopted in 1603 after the governments of England and Scotland had been joined, under the name of Great Britain and the leadership of King James. It superimposed Scotland's blue-and-white Cross of St. Andrew over England's red-and-white Cross of St. George. For longer-range identification, the ship's prows and afterdecks were painted bright geometric designs, which revealed them to be not men-of-war but merchantmen. In case of attack by Spaniards, Portuguese, or pirates they carried deck guns of limited range, several of which were destined to protect the fort the settlers were to build in Virginia.

Preparation for the voyage did not escape Spain, though the two nations technically had been at peace since 1604. In a coded message from London in 1606, Spain's ambassador warned his king, Philip III: "They propose to do another thing, which is to send five or six hundred men, private individuals of this kingdom, to people Virginia in the Indies, close to Florida." The ambassador also confronted Sir John Popham, Chief Justice of England, with this report and informed him that such a settlement would encroach on Spanish territory and violate the treaty. The Chief Justice explained that he favored the expedition only to rid England of thieves by drowning them.

However, prospect of a Virginia settlement so alarmed Philip that he asked his councilors how to deal with it. When the Spanish Board of War of the Indies advised that "With all necessary forces this plan of

The extensive settlement area granted to the Virginia Company of London by King James in 1606 was increased in the second charter of 1609 to run "from sea to sea." *Map by William Gravitt adapted from "A Hornbook of Virginia History"*

200 Miles
Old Point
Comfort
200 Miles

The three ships bearing Virginia's 105 first settlers sailed from Blackwall docks on the Thames River at London on December 20, 1606. Sir Walter Raleigh remained imprisoned in the Tower of London, at right. *National Park Service*

The merchant ships that brought the settlers to Virginia were similar to the heavy-timbered vessels shown in these seventeenth-century drawings. *Colonial Williamsburg*

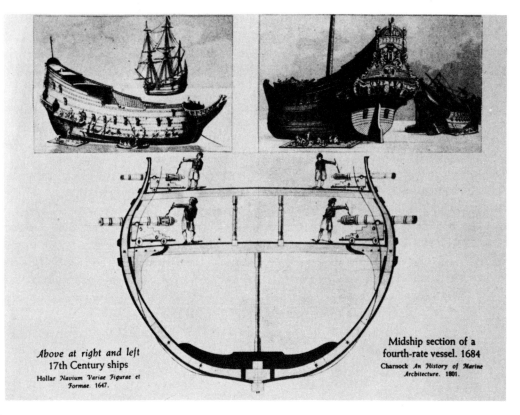

Above at right and left
17th Century ships
Hollar *Navium Variae Figurae et Formae.* 1647.

Midship section of a fourth-rate vessel. 1684
Charnock *An History of Marine Architecture.* 1801.

THE VOYAGE, AS DESCRIBED BY GEORGE PERCY

1. December 20, 1606, "the fleet fell from London."
2. February 12, 1607, "we saw a blazing Starre, and presently a storme."
3. March 23, "we fell with the Illand Mattanenio (Martinique)."
4. April 10, "we set saile and disimboged (departed) out of the West Indies and bare oure course Northerly."
5. April 26, "wee descried the Land of Virginia (and) wee entred into the Bay of Chesupioc (Chesapeake)."
6. May 13, "we came to our seating place (Jamestown Island) where oure shippes doe lie so neere the shoare that they are moored to the trees."
7. May 14, "we landed all our men, which were set to worke about the fortification."

The South Atlantic route chosen by Captain Newport to reach Virginia took the vessels almost to South America before they turned north toward Chesapeake Bay. *The Jamestown Foundation*

the English should be prevented," King Philip had his ambassador in London obtain an audience with King James and present objections. James I promised only to "look into the matter," and the offended ambassador advised Philip to drive the English out of Virginia, "hanging them in time which is short enough for the purpose."

Philip's councilors also urged that he send a naval force against Virginia, but Philip refused to act. Perhaps memory of the Armada was still too strong. Whatever the cause, Spain missed her chance in 1606-07 to destroy the seed of England in the New World at the moment of planting. She was to regret her indecision.

Newport's seamanship brought the three ships together to Virginia with loss of only one of the 105 settlers and none of the 39

sailors who had embarked on the outbound tide at Blackwall. Contrary winds first forced them to anchor six weeks in the Downs, along the English Channel, but early in February, 1607, the winds shifted, and Newport in the *Susan Constant* made signal to Gosnold in the *Godspeed* and Captain John Ratcliffe in the *Discovery* to set sail.

The route was the usual one in the south Atlantic: southward along the coast of France and Spain and thence to the Canary Islands for fresh water. Reaching the Tropic of Cancer, the ships veered away from the African coast and safely crossed the Atlantic to the island of Martinique. They were then three months out of London. Two-thirds of their journey was behind them.

Carefully threading their way through

the Caribbean to avoid confrontation by Spanish warships, they stopped in turn at Dominica, Guadeloupe, Nevis, and Mona. On the last tiny island died Edward Brooke, first of the 105 settlers to meet death. Colonist George Percy, son of the Duke of Northumberland, recorded in his diary that Brooke's "fat melted within him by the great heat and drought of the country." After a lingering farewell to the island of Monito, the refreshed sailors turned north on the most crucial leg of the journey.

Guided only by the stars, by experience, and by the simplest of navigational aides, Newport and Gosnold must make their landfall on schedule or risk a shortage of food and water. A spring squall hit the ships, and they lowered sail to avoid being grounded, believing themselves in Virginia's shoal waters. Their hopes were premature, however, and they sailed five more days before they saw its headlands.

"The sixth and twentieth day of April," wrote Percy, "about four o'clock in the morning, we descried the Land of Virginia; the same day we entered the bay of Chesupioc directly." The day was Sunday, April 26, 1607. As the sun rose over black waters, sailors could discern the low, pine-forested shore of Virginia.

Landing a few men on a peninsula, they cautiously explored the rim of Chesapeake Bay. The dogwood and redbud were at their springtime best. Wild strawberries covered the ground, and the land abounded in strange plants, birds, and animals. Percy was entranced with "fair meadows and goodly tall trees, with such fresh-waters running through the woods as I was almost ravished at the first sight thereof." But pleasure turned to pain when Indians emerged and drove the exploring party back aboardship, wounding settler Gabriel Archer and sailor Matthew Morton. Such was the first Virginians' welcome to Virginia.

On their arrival at the Virginia capes, the settlers erected a cross and the Rev. Robert Hunt, their chaplain, conducted a service of thanksgiving. *Norfolk Museum of Arts and Sciences*

The coat of arms of the Virginia Company of London hailed the colony as "the fifth part" of the King's dominions. The others were England and Wales, considered as one; France, Scotland, and Ireland. *From "A Hornbook of Virginia History"*

Arrival of the settlers at Jamestown on May 13, 1607, was fancifully portrayed in a contemporary print. Indians opposed the colony. *American Heritage Publishing Co., Inc.*

During the 16 weeks under sail Newport had been the unquestioned master of the three ships, the 39 seamen, and the settlers, now reduced to 104. At Cape Henry the sealed instructions of the company were opened, and Newport was forced to share leadership for the rest of the voyage with his fellow captains, Gosnold and Ratcliffe, together with settlers Edward Maria Wingfield, John Martin, George Kendall, and that most controversial hero of American legend, Captain John Smith. No longer would Newport exercise simple military command. Hereafter he must abide by the wishes of the quarrelsome Council.

Thus, in Virginia's scented April, the argonauts reached the land that Drayton had called "earth's only paradise." So rich and numerous were its charms that they were filled with the desire to hasten ashore and find the riches which must abound in so favored a country.

But instructions from His Majesty's Council for Virginia, handed to the leaders before they sailed from London, had directed the colonists to look westward in search of the rumored passage to the "South Sea," and to establish themselves so far inland from the Atlantic that coast-watchers might warn the colony by runner if Spanish marauders should approach from the sea. Accordingly, the three ships lifted anchor and hoisted sail to explore the most westerly of the rivers in the Chesapeake basin, seeking the best place to plant the capital of the new English nation.

On May 13, 1607, after examining all deepwater sites along the river as far west as its fall line, they chose a wooded peninsula extending well out toward the channel. There they wearily moored their ships to the limbs of overhanging trees and slept aboardship for their last night before moving their goods and chattels ashore. Being loyal Englishmen, they named the river the James and their settlement James Town, for their King. It was to be the rooting place of English civilization in the New World and the beginning of a migration that was to make Great Britain the most powerful force in the world.

Close by the site of Jamestown, and unknown to its settlers, were the remains of a mission that the Spanish had sought to plant in the Chesapeake Bay area 37 years earlier. In the autumn of 1570 a ship from the fleet of General Pedro de Menendez, founder of St. Augustine, had explored the waterway and named it The Bay of the Mother of God. Their records indicate that they, too, sailed up the westerly river now called the James. Two miles downriver from the later site of Jamestown, they turned into a creek and approached the present site of Williamsburg. There they landed nine Jesuit missionaries, who hoped to Christianize the

John Smith recorded results of his exploration of Virginia from 1607 to 1609 in this map. Locations of Indian tribes and villages show the extent of Powhatan's kingdom. *Colonial Williamsburg*

Indians in a mission along the present Felgate Creek, a tributary of the York River. But Indians massacred all except one of the settlers, who was rescued by a Spanish relief ship in 1572. Thus had ended Spain's efforts to settle north of Florida.

At Jamestown England finally realized her ambition for a foothold in the New World. The settling of Virginia would change the history of mankind.

Arrival of the first permanent English settlers off Jamestown Island, May 13, 1607

3 Raleigh's Vision of a New English Nation

OVERLEAF: The Arrival of Lord de la Warr . *From photograph of diorama by Tom Williams. National Park Service.*

CHANGING ATTITUDES IN THE COLONY: *The political leaders wanted to extend British power and exploit the new lands; the commoners saw prospects of wealth and freer living. Both shared the expanding national ambition fed by the achievements of explorers and naval captains. Virginia's settlers conformed to the political and religious principles of the British majority and thus differed from the Puritan and Roman Catholic minorities that wanted religious independence. But the settlers of Virginia, supporters of a King whose powers were limited by the ruling aristocracy, also brought a distrust of repression and a strong bias for individual freedom.*

3

Raleigh's Vision of a New English Nation

Virginia was settled to extend British power and to enrich British trade. Moralizers a century ago deplored its lack of spiritual motivation, but a more realistic age recognizes that its pioneers' quest for independence was one of the important forces of modern history. It is true that its settlers were not held together by a minority consciousness, like the Puritans in Massachusetts or the Baptists later in Rhode Island. They had admittedly no burning desire to change the world or to convert the heathen Indian to Christianity, as the Spanish tried hard to do in their colonies, with sometimes questionable results.

Instead, Virginia was from its beginning a faithful replica of England and her attitudes, which were frankly monarchistic, capitalistic, class-conscious, and tolerantly Anglican in religion. They were the same attitudes that enabled England to colonize and govern, with reasonable progress and stability, the greatest empire in history for the next 200 years.

Early Virginia shared the virtues and vices of England, and — for better or worse — Virginia helped to spread them generously over the great part of North America where Virginia's influence was strong in America's first two and a half centuries.

Virginians were evangelists for England — not members of a minority who had moved away from English shores in protest against real or fancied evils.

Virginia's social structure in the first years of the settlement was the stratified structure that prevailed in England in 1607. Of the 92 first settlers whom Smith and others recorded by name, 49 are designated as "gentlemen," occupying a privileged place in pitifully primitive Jamestown. This meant that they were neither tradesmen, professional men, nor members of the nobility. For this overabundance of gentility, the colony was to pay dearly in its early years, until those who were unable to adjust had died, been killed by Indians, or given up and gone home. But the leadership and standards of educated men were accepted from the beginning at Jamestown. They were part of a political and economic enterprise which in 175 years was to produce a new nation of unprecedented scope, built on English foundations.

The interest that England's political leaders and merchants took in Virginia gave the settlement broader support in 1606 than Raleigh had achieved and assured its success. The 1606 charter listed only eight of the prospective adventurers and omits the two presumed leaders, Chief Justice Sir John Popham and the businessman Sir Thomas Smythe, who arranged the financing. However, when the charter was amended and re-issued by the King in 1609 it carried the names of all 650 investors. Among them were 50 of the London merchant companies, the Lord Mayor of London, Shakespeare's patron, the Earl of Southampton, leading clergymen, and such independent Parliamentary spirits as Sir Edwin Sandys, who did not fear to defy King James himself. Such powerful backing gave Virginia needed strength at the hour of her birth.

In the nature of Virginia's settlers was the expectation of the freedom they had known in their relation with their govern-

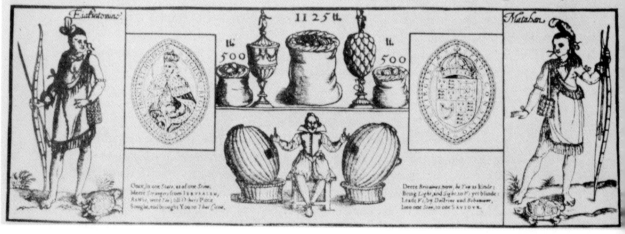

The Virginia Company in 1615 conducted this lottery to raise funds for the settlement.
Virginia Historical Society

James Fort, a triangular palisade, was built to house the colonists at Jamestown. Around the church were a guardhouse, a storehouse and fifteen dwellings. *National Park Service*

ment, in their business, and in their spiritual life. By twentieth century American standards their concept of their political rights was limited, but it was evolving steadily under the influence of Magna Carta, the Protestant Reformation, scientific inquiry, and the growing acceptance of the rule of law at every level of life.

The strong middle class which had grown up in medieval England helped build this quality into a nation of increasing political maturity. They were willing to be led but refused to be coerced. Its members were skeptical of government, as Virginians were always to be. They had known the evils of unrestrained monarchy, selfish nobles, and a clergy out of touch with its times. To correct these, they had succes-

sively restrained the powers of king, nobility, and of the Church's hierarchy. While they had the free-born Englishman's confidence that he was inherently as good as anybody, they accepted the class system because in England – unlike the Continent – social strata were fluid enough to allow for the rise of the talented, the ambitious, and the worthy.

Each settler in his heart felt that with fair opportunity he could grow wealthy and gain his rightful station in society. It was this desire for a better place in life which made Englishmen cross menacing seas to Virginia. In the words of Captain Seagull of *Eastward Ho*, "For your means to advancement, there it is simple and not preposterously mixed. You may be an alderman

Raleigh's Vision of a New English Nation   [59]

there, and never be scavenger; you may be any other officer, and never be slave." The charter of the London Company granted to Virginia's settlers all the liberties, franchises, and immunities enjoyed by Englishmen in England. But Virginia's vastness was the greatest promise.

England was able to plant a colony in Virginia because of four historic developments. First, she had a confidence that grew out of her triumph over Spain in 1588. Second, her people realized that her growth as a major power would depend on the accumulation of territory and on trade with undeveloped lands. Third, her businessmen had created in the stock company an instrument through which the slowly-accumulating capital of the new industrial age could be used to settle these new territories and create new enterprises. Finally, England had liberated scholarship from control by the clergy, freeing her intellectual energies for the development of science and industry. Long after King Henry VIII had removed secular matters from control of the hierarchy in England, other European nations were hampered by the ecclesiastical involvement in civil government.

Free inquiry thus enjoyed a head start in sixteenth century England and was an incentive to explore the world. English America was to reject the concept of the divine right of kings and encourage the rise of Parliament and a division of powers between the King, the lords, the commons, and the courts.

Popular sentiment in England also discouraged religious absolutism of the Papal sort and led to an Anglican Church which permitted a wide latitude in discipline (and a lesser latitude in dogma) within its communion. Confinement of the Church to spiritual and educational matters was accepted practice in England by the time Virginia was settled. It led to a very different colony at Jamestown from the theocracy that the Puritans planted later in Massachusetts.

The relationship between church and state that evolved in Virginia was to result after the American Revolution in Thomas Jefferson's Statute for Religious Freedom, in the guarantee of freedom of conscience and worship written into the United States Constitution, and in the disestablishment of the Anglican Church by action of the legislatures in Virginia and other original states. From the limited "toleration" that the colonial government of Virginia accorded Presbyterians and Quakers and later to Lutherans, Methodists, and Baptists, public sentiment has gradually forced complete separation of church and state in America.

Despite strong backing, the effort to plant a colony in Virginia in 1607 proved nearly fatal. The immense project was under-financed, and the sponsors were too anxious for profit. Discord flourished, and few of the "knight adventurers" were capable of the hard and bloody tasks required for survival. For nearly ten years the settlers clung to the shore of the James like invaders holding an enemy beachhead. Only the introduction of tobacco culture in 1612 saved the colony, by encouraging stockholders in England with the prospect of a return on their investment.

The morning after their arrival, the settlers began to stake out the triangular wooden stockade which was to be Virginia's hub. While the Council elected Edward Maria Wingfield president, other settlers cleared a site and cut clapboard as cargo for the ships' return voyage. In a few days English wheat, oats, and barley were sprouting in small clearings around the camp. A wattle-and-daub church, a storehouse, a guardhouse, and fifteen simple houses were erected inside the fort. Captain Newport saw his passengers safely surrounded by a palisade and then set sail on June 22 for England, leaving the pinnace *Discovery* behind for the search for a passage to the South Sea.

The colonists' ordeal began promptly with the onset of Virginia's summer. It grew worse as worms infested their grain, water casks ran dry, and an epidemic killed half the settlers, leaving men "night and day groaning in every corner of the Fort most pitiful to hear." In September President Wingfield was deposed and succeeded for a brief year by John Ratcliffe, who proved no abler to command. At last the Council recognized the most energetic and resource-

Captain John Smith was the third and ablest of Jamestown's early Governors. *Colonial Williamsburg*

Ætatis suæ 21. Aᵒ. 1616.

Matoaks als Rebecka daughter to the mighty Prince Powhatan Emperour of Attanoughkomouck als Virginia converted and baptized in the Christian faith, and Wife to the worᵗʰ Mʳ Thoː Rolff.

The Indian Princess Pocohontas befriended Virginia's settlers. *Mellon Collection, National Portrait Gallery*

ful of its members, electing John Smith as president. Virginia by this time had been reinforced by Newport in two supply voyages and numbered 500, including its first women, Mrs. Forrest and her maid, Ann Burras, who married John Laydon in the first recorded English wedding in America. Food and shelter were urgently needed for the winter.

The choice of Smith gave hope, for he had served as soldier in Hungary, Turkey, and Transylvania and knew how to survive. He had landed in Virginia in chains, accused of mutiny, but his appointment to the Council had freed him to explore the tidal creeks and rivers, meeting the Indians and trading for food. Like Raleigh, he was a man of action, imbued with the ideal of service to King and country, and like Raleigh he was

Raleigh's Vision of a New English Nation [61]

a skilled writer, sending to England in 1608 a letter which saw publication as *A True Relation* and provided the clearest picture of Virginia until his *General History of Virginia* was printed in 1624. In the latter Smith told of being saved by the lovely Princess Pocahontas after he had been condemned to death by Chief Powhatan. The tale delighted endless generations. It was apparently true, but it raised endless questions of his veracity.

Although Smith shared the Elizabethan taste for boasting, his brisk leadership pumped life into the colony. On one hand he was obliged to satisfy investors, who demanded a search for gold and profitable exports, and on the other the settlers' need for food, shelter, security, and a sense of direction.

George Percy was the son of the Duke of Northumberland. He kept a diary of the settlement. *Colonial Williamsburg*

Captain John Smith's *General History of Virginia, New England, and the Summer Isles* contains the account of his rescue by Pocahontas from her father's wrath. *Central Office of Information, London*

Like most Englishmen of his day, he was no more than five feet tall, but he had a bantam's cockiness. As the least educated member of the Council, he felt himself obliged to prove the equal of the others, and his writings and maps of Virginia and later of New England show him a man of wide knowledge. Handsome and full-bearded, he boasted of his prowess with the ladies but never took a wife. His writings spread Virginia's fame and lured settlers who kept Virginia alive.

Other able men were among the first settlers. The Rev. Robert Hunt, a graduate of Oxford and chaplain to the colony, faith-

Jamestown was built on a peninsula that jutted into the James River forty miles above the entrance to the Virginia Capes. *National Park Service*

New settlers built homes outside the palisade as fears of attack by the Spaniards and the Indians decreased. James Fort at the right. *Jamestown Foundation*

fully ministered to others until his early death at Jamestown. From his ministry until the American Revolution, the English church was to be a part of Virginia and of America. Captain Bartholomew Gosnold, an alumnus of Cambridge, had surveyed the New England coast in 1602, discovered and named Cape Cod, and given his daughter's name to Martha's Vineyard. He too died in Virginia, in 1607.

Captain Gabriel Archer, a product of the Inns of Court, was the first lawyer in Virginia, and Captain John Martin, son of a three-term Lord Mayor of London, had sailed around the world with Sir Francis Drake and had accompanied Sir Richard Grenville's expedition to relieve the ill-fated Roanoke Island colony. He patented Martin's Brandon 20 miles upriver from Jamestown and lived there until his death in 1632, one of the few to survive the first three years. The most nobly-born of the settlers was George Percy, younger son of the Duke of Northumberland, who served as a member of the Council from 1607 until he returned to England in 1612.

The settlement from 1608 to 1611 progressed from crisis to crisis. Despite John Smith's vigorous husbandry, the winter of 1609-10 was a starving time, and the populace shrank from 500 to 50. Then Smith was injured by gunpowder and forced to return to England. A relief force sent from England was shipwrecked in Bermuda, and when Lieutenant Governor Sir Thomas Gates finally arrived in May, 1610, he found the settlers so weak and dispirited that he loaded them aboard ship to return to England. Only the arrival of Governor Lord De la Warr on June 10 in the lower James River, with supplies and 150 new settlers, forestalled this intended desertion.

Fear of attack by troops from the Spanish outpost in Florida was constantly in the settlers' mind, and a lookout for ships was kept atop the bulwarks of James Fort. On Newport's return to London after the 1607 voyage, he took letters asking reinforcement against "the all-devouring Spaniard." In *A Prayer Said Upon the Court of Guard* in James Fort, the settlers bravely repeated the words: "We know, O Lord, we have the Devil and all the gates of Hell against us, but if Thou, O Lord, be on our side, we care not who be against us." Recognizing their impotence amid so many dangers, they asked: "And, seeing by Thy motion and work in our hearts, we have left our warm nest at home and put our lives into Thy hands, principally to honor Thy name and advance the Kingdom of Thy Son, Lord give us leave to commit our lives into Thy hands."

While Spain came close, she never struck. A Spanish ship sailed from St. Augustine to Chesapeake Bay in 1609 but turned back at the sight of an English vessel. The Spanish ambassador in London advised his King in 1610 that English enthusiasm for Virginia was cooling. The Spanish Council of State recommended that ships be sent to destroy Jamestown the next spring, but King Philip, with characteristic caution, held back.

Secret intelligence also flowed from the English ambassador in Spain to King James I. In 1611 he wrote that Spanish ships were ready to strike Virginia, but he doubted the "poor ability" of Spain. When this report was passed to Virginia, the settlers strengthened their defense by building a blockhouse on Hog Island, four miles below Jamestown, with a tower from which a sentinel could warn of danger. To serve as an inland retreat, John Smith before his departure in 1609 directed construction of a fort across the James in Surry, to which settlers could retire in such case. Fortunately, it was not needed.

Jamestown's principal outpost, however, remained at Fort Algernon, built in 1609 at Point Comfort on the Chesapeake Bay "for the commodious discovery of any shipping which should come upon the coast." Only once was it threatened. In 1611 a large Spanish caravel, accompanied by a smaller shallop, dropped anchor outside the fort's range and sent three men ashore, allegedly to seek a Spanish ship lost on its way to the West Indies. Obtaining the services of an English pilot, John Clark, to bring their ship into harbor, the Spanish agreed to leave three of their men behind as hostages and then sailed with the surprised Clark to Spain.

One of the Spaniards, Diego de Molina, was held for four years as a prisoner-at-large in Virginia before being returned to England in 1615 under care of Captain John Martin. Molina's diagram of James Fort, spirited back to Spain, is one of the few visual records of early Jamestown.

Wearying of finding gold or a sea passage to the west, the Virginians turned to other efforts. Eight Germans and Poles were brought over to produce glass, and other artisans were encouraged to make other items needed in England. A glass factory was built on the mainland adjoining the Jamestown peninsula, and iron was forged, barrels were made, timber and clapboard hewn, and pitch and tar processed and sent back to England.

None of Jamestown's exports was to excite the English market, however, until a serious-minded settler named John Rolfe

The early settlers at Jamestown erected structures with high peaked roofs covered with thatch. This is the reconstructed glass factory of 1608, where bottles and other glass objects were blown. *The Jamestown Foundation*

Tobacco proved to be Virginia's chief source of livelihood in the seventeenth and eighteenth centuries. This early German print shows methods of cultivation similar to Jamestown's. *Arents Collection, New York Public Library*

obtained seed in 1611 or 1612 from a ship captain who had put into port at Trinidad, a Spanish possession. Harvested first in 1612, Rolfe's big yellow leaf proved popular in England, which had been importing tobacco from Spain in increasing quantity since Sir Walter Raleigh had introduced pipe smoking at Queen Elizabeth's court twenty-five years earlier.

Demand for Virginia tobacco developed, and investors in the Virginia Company began to take heart. By 1619 more than 40,000 pounds of tobacco a year were shipped to

England. Talk of tobacco farming brought more settlers to Virginia, and new plantations were established along the James River. Virginia was beginning to take root.

In 1612 John Rolfe grew the first crop of Spanish tobacco at Jamestown. Its popularity in England insured the colony's success. *Sidney King for The Jamestown Foundation*

4   What England Brought to Virginia

Indians attacked the English one early March morning in 1622 and killed 349 of Virginia's 1,250 settlers. *Colonial Williamsburg*

OVERLEAF: Settlement soon spread from Jamestown across the James River. St. Luke's Church was built beginning about 1632 near the present Smithfield. It still stands. *Historic St. Luke's Restoration*

BETWEEN KING AND PARLIAMENT: *James I takes control of English colonies out of the hands of the merchant companies. Virginia develops a tobacco enonomy and is freer politically during the Cromwellian Revolution. Opinion splits between the conservative Tories and the more liberal Whigs. Changing fortunes at Jamestown during Governor Berkeley's two administrations and the people's protest in Bacon's Rebellion.*

What England Brought to Virginia

Virginia grew. Settlers dared move out of James Fort now to build homes along Jamestown's paths or on the banks of neighboring creeks. Jamestown became a village of narrow wooden row-houses following the meandering course of its cart roads. By 1612 the colony had reached a population of 800, most of them men, and another settlement was beginning at Kecoughtan, near the guns of Fort Algernon, in the present city of Hampton. Governor Sir Thomas Dale saw need for a capital farther up the James, and he selected a peninsula at Dutch Gap, near the present Richmond. There he had settlers build a new palisade, a blockhouse, and homes to accommodate 300, calling it Henricus to honor King James' son, Prince Henry.

A University of Henrico was proposed, and the Virginia Company pledged 10,000 acres for its use. The industrious Dale also founded other settlements on the James at Bermuda and Shirley Hundred.

Peace with the Indians encouraged growth. John Rolfe in 1614 married the 18-year-old Indian princess Pocahontas in the presence of Governor Dale, a handful of Pocahontas' people, and the Spanish spy Molina. The effect of this union on the 9000 tribesmen governed by her father, Chief Powhatan, might have been permanent peace had not Pocahontas died three years later at Gravesend, England, while returning with Rolfe and their infant son Thomas after presentation at court. A year after her un-

Governor Sir Thomas Dale in 1612 planned the new Virginia capital of Henricus near Richmond, but it did not replace Jamestown. *The Williams Fund, Virginia Museum of Fine Arts*

RIGHT: Sir Edwin Sandys was chosen head of the Virginia Company of London in 1618 in a stockholders' purge of Sir Thomas Smythe's administration.

timely death the aged Powhatan himself died, transferring power over the Indians to the aggressive Chief Opechancanough.

The accession of the new chief was disastrous for Virginia. John Smith had written of the Indians, "Some are of disposition fearful, some bold, some cautelous, all savage," and Opechancanough proved most savage of all. By his orders, naked warriors fell upon Virginia households in the early morning on Good Friday, in 1622, and killed 349 of Virginia's 1,250 settlers. Jamestown itself was saved, having been warned by a friendly Indian youth, Chanco. Ironically, one of the victims appears to have been John

Rolfe. His son Thomas remained at school in England and thereby lived to perpetuate a Virginia family second in age in English America only to the family lines left by Robert Beheathland and William Spencer, who alone of the first 104 settlers of Virginia are known to have descendants.

The military rule of Jamestown's early years violated the promise of full British rights to the settlers, and resentment developed as the colony gained strength. Some company officials were sympathetic, and these took advantage of conflict among the stockholders to gain power and make changes. Sir Thomas Smythe, who had headed the company, was blamed for early disappointments. In 1612 dissatisfied stockholders amended the London Company charter to give his office less power and themselves more by having more frequent company meetings.

Smythe and his fellow London businessmen, who because of their closeness to the King were known as the Court Party, thus came into conflict with stockholders outside London, known as the Country Party. A quarrel broke out between Smythe and Lord Rich, afterward the Earl of Warwick. In 1618 Warwick and his Country Party adherents replaced Smythe as treasurer with Sir Edwin Sandys, a liberal member of Parliament from rural England.

Under Sandys' leadership the London Company began to move toward self-government in Virginia. At its quarterly "court" on November 28, 1618, it ratified a more democratic order in *The Great Charter of Privileges, Orders, and Laws* and dispatched Governor Sir George Yeardley to James-

town with instructions to convene a General Assembly.

In response to Yeardley's call, an election was duly held, and two Burgesses from each of the eleven principal localities in Virginia gathered at Jamestown on July 30, 1619, and met in the choir stalls of the new wooden church outside the deserted remains of James Fort.

This was the first legislative body to meet in the New World. For the next 150 years it was to try valiantly to obtain for colonists in Virginia the rights which they believed due every Englishman wherever he might live. In seeking such rights, Virginia's Assemblymen were joining an evolutionary movement that had been under way in England for 400 years, gradually circumscribing the powers of king and nobles while enlarging the rights of the comman man. The eventual revolt of Virginia and the other American colonies occurred because neither King nor Parliament would concede to colonists the rights of native Englishmen.

John Rolfe in 1614 married Pocahontas. The union encouraged peace between Englishmen and Indians until after her death three years later in England. *Colonial Williamsburg*

The Virginia Assembly that met in the church at Jamestown on July 30, 1619, was the first representative legislative body in the New World. *Life Insurance Co. of Virginia*

The rise of parliamentary government in Virginia followed that of England. This, the earliest picture of England's House of Commons, shows the last session of Parliament of King James I in 1624. Sir Edwin Sandys was active in both efforts. *Office of Information, London*

The beginning of Virginia's political life in 1619 was made possible by the infusion of strength from tobacco cultivation. While self-government was to come slowly, Sandys was wise enough to see that England in Virginia demanded some measure of political growth if it was to thrive. Under Sandys' leadership, the company in 1619 further stimulated Virginians' permanence and ambition by awarding a grant of land to each settler. "Ancient Planters" who had come in the first nine years each received 100 acres, while subsequent arrivals received 50 acres plus an additional 50 for each person brought over. Another practical step was the dispatch by the company of a shipload of young women, or "maids," to become wives for settlers who paid for their transportation. A few women had preceded them to Jamestown, beginning with the arrival in 1608 of Mrs. Forrest and her maid, Ann Burras.

Though conditions in the colony improved, those in the company worsened. As sickening accounts of the Massacre of 1622 reached London, a new pamphlet attacking the colony's management was published in London under title of *The Unmasked Face of our Colony in Virginia.* It gave the King a basis, though flimsy, to smite Sir Edwin Sandys and other Parliamentary critics who resented James I's efforts to buy peace with Spain by marrying Prince Charles to the Spanish Infanta.

Formal complaint was lodged against the Virginia Company in the King's Privy Council. In defense of the company's management, Governor Sir Francis Wyatt, his Council of State, and the Virginia Assembly sent to London a *Tragical Declaration of the Virginia Assembly,* which hotly defended the company's management. Rather than submit again to such government as Sir Thomas Smythe's regime had sent before Yeardley's arrival, they wrote, "We desire His Majesty that commissioners may be sent over with authority to hang us."

Logic in this case was on the King's side, however. As increasing numbers of his subjects crossed the Atlantic to the new world of Virginia, a clear line of authority must be established from Great Britain's government to Jamestown's. The King's Attorney General recommended that Virginia become a royal province, no longer responsive to the London Company, and the Privy Council concurred. They proposed that the King rather than the company should henceforth appoint the resident Council for Virginia in London, the Governor, and his Council of State. London Company stockholders pleaded with Parliament to protect their investment, but the King forbade Parliament to act. He announced that British colonies overseas would thereafter be governed by the King and his Privy Council. This was to remain Royal policy in America.

Had England far-sightedly provided at this moment that Virginia should be represented on the Privy Council and in Parliament, as was later done with Scotland and Northern Ireland, a link might have been formed between England and America too strong to be broken. However, Parliament had not yet acquired sufficient power in 1624 to dictate to the Crown on such an issue. Virginia's settlers and stockholders were therefore powerless against the ruling of the Lord Chief Justice that "the patent or charter of the Company of English Merchants trading to Virginia, and pretending to exercise a power and authority over His Majesty's good subjects there, should be henceforth null and void."

The contest for control of Virginia was an episode in the long struggle between James I and his Stuart successors, on the one hand, and the growing confidence of Parliament on the other. From this contest, Virginians were to gain courage as the rights of Englishmen were gradually extended, in response to pressure from the House of Commons. From the authoritarian control of absolute rulers, British government slowly evolved into more democratic form, whose initiative rested with the people and their elected government.

Sir Edwin Sandys was an early leader in this movement, arousing King James' hostility to the point that the King urged Virginia Company stockholders in their election of a treasurer in 1619 to "choose the Devil if you will, but not Sir Edwin Sandys." After the Chief Justice's nullification of the company charter in 1624, company records from the time of Sandys' election were ordered destroyed. However, an unauthorized copy was later smuggled to Virginia. It was in possession of Thomas Jefferson when his library was acquired in 1814 as the nucleus of the Library of Congress.

Virginia's statehouse remained at Jamestown until 1699. A succession of Governors was appointed by the crown, but the majority remained in London to lobby at Court and sent other men as Lieutenant Governors to Virginia in their stead. Such was the Lieutenant Governor's prestige as the King's representative that relations between Virginia and Great Britain directly reflected his popularity. Instead of the early guarantee that they enjoyed the "rights, privileges, and immunities" of resident Englishmen, the colonists now had their political rights re-defined by the monarch in instructions sent with each Governor to Virginia.

Jamestown was a small and simple town to be capital of so vast an area. At its height it had less than a thousand residents. It was chiefly distinguished by its accessibility to the maze of creeks feeding the broad James, which served boatmen as the highway of colonial Virginia. It also symbolized the presence of the King's authority in the person of the Governor or Lieutenant Governor, who represented the King, governed the Church in Virginia, commanded the military, dealt with Indians and with other colonies, enforced laws, dispensed jobs, nominated his friends for appointment by the King to the Council of State and other offices, and sat as presiding officer of the Council in making and enforcing laws and in punishing the noncompliant.

The chief opportunity for Virginians to make themselves heard came in the annual sitting of the Assembly at Jamestown. In the General Assembly's first years the elected delegate's voice was diminished by the fact that the Governor and his appointed Council sat and voted in one body with the Burgesses. At length, in 1651, the Assembly divided into two houses, the lower taking the name of the House of Burgesses and the upper the Governor's Council of State.

These annual sittings were known as Public Times and drew officials from all parts of the colony to deliberate in the Assembly, to try causes arising under the law, and then to adjourn to Jamestown's rustic homes and taverns to quaff ale, play cards, and talk over issues of the day.

For so large a territory, Virginia's governmental establishment was small. Like the rural England from which most Virginians emigrated, the colony was a farming country of few villages and little commerce, except for the tobacco shipped on board British and Dutch sailing ships and the manufactured goods brought back in return. Like the rural residents of England who made up the Country Party, its people were mistrustful of the merchants who clustered in London and plied the Court for favors. As the Country Party evolved into the Whigs and the Court Party into the Tories, Virginia sentiment naturally supported the Whigs, who shared the Virginia farmers' mistrust of royal power and of the influence of London businessmen on government.

Except for a scattering of merchants in the port towns, most Virginians were pro-Whig by the time of the Revolution Settlement of 1688 in England. In this declaration of Whig principles, the growing Parliamentary power decreed that thereafter no legislation could be passed, taxation could be levied, or armed forces could be maintained in Great Britain without the authority of Parliament. The political philosopher John Locke became the spokesman for Whigs and most Virginians when he wrote and published his two *Treatises on Civil Government* in 1688, advocating constitutional government and religious toleration for England. Locke anticipated Thomas Jefferson and the American revolutionaries with his declaration that all men were equal and independent in the original state of nature and that no man had the right to harm another.

In addition to the Governor or Lieutenant Governor, the Virginia colony's officials at Jamestown were the Secretary of State, who was appointed by the King on recommendation of the Governor and who in turn appointed Clerks of the County Courts; the Public Treasurer, who received taxes and special duties on skins, furs, liquors, slaves, and indentured servants; and the Clerk of the General Assembly, who was appointed by that body.

Outside Jamestown the ranking officials were Justices of the Peace, who were judges of the county courts. The Justices had primary jurisdiction in most cases and meted out punishment by stocks, whipping post, pillory, ducking stool, or incarceration in

An eighteenth century British tobacco label depicts the Englishman's conception of life in the tobacco-growing colonies. The seller's slogan is "The Best Tobacco Under the Sun." *Central Office of Information, London*

jail. They also discharged other non-judicial responsibilities which in later centuries were assumed by county boards of supervisors and city councils. Justices of the Peace were appointed by the Governor with the advice of the Council of State, which served for most of Virginia's first century as its highest court.

On a defendant's request he could be heard by a jury of his peers under the protection of Magna Carta. Should he be convicted, he could appeal to the General Court, consisting of the Governor and Council, at its quarterly session at Jamestown. The General Assembly heard appeals in some cases.

At the local level of government, one Justice of the Peace in each county had additional responsibility as Sheriff, whose chief function was to collect taxes. Other county officers were King's Attorneys, Constables, Clerks, and Coroners, all appointed by the Governor and Council. Within the county were parishes, whose lines were so drawn that their parishioners were accessible to church. Within each parish a vestry was responsible for the spiritual life of its people and the care of the poor and unfortunate. However, because of sparse population and lack of ministers, some parishes went unchurched.

Because both civil and religious authorities were appointed by the crown, they were expected to work together for the public good. Churchwardens were required to "deliver a true presentment in writing of such misdemeanors as to their knowledge have been committed" in the previous year. Failure to attend worship consistently was punishable by law. A judge might discipline an offender by sentencing him to make public confession in a church. Public office was restricted to those who accepted Anglican belief and took part in the life of the church. Despite the important role which the church played in seventeenth century Virginia, however, there were few instances of intemperate treatment of freethinkers except during the latter period of the governorship of Sir William Berkeley.

For most of the ninety-two years when Jamestown was capital, the initiative in Virginia political affairs rested with the Governor. However, during the tenure of Berkeley, which extended from 1642 to 1677, the colonists successfully asserted the right to introduce their own legislation into the Assembly. England's preoccupation with her Civil War from 1652 to 1661 loosened her hold on Virginia and gave the colonists many political advantages, which they never entirely gave up. Berkeley and his government resigned in 1652, after the Parliamentary forces of Oliver Cromwell took control in England. For seven years Virginia virtually governed herself, while England seethed. Berkeley returned to office in 1661 when Royal control was restored, but neither he nor the office was ever the same.

Virginia made great strides in the first flush of Berkeley's governorship. Succeeding to the office on the removal of Sir John Harvey, the new executive was vigorous, effective, and popular. He dealt decisively with Virginia's Indians after the massacre of 1644, protected Virginia's western boundaries and territorial claims, sent expeditions north and west to trade and strengthen Virginia's claim to the Ohio Valley, and held Virginia loyal to the exiled King Charles II and his Cavaliers during the seven years of England's Civil War.

After the Cromwellian interregnum, King Charles II reappointed the faithful

Governor Sir William Berkeley served longer than any governor in Virginia's first century and had greater influence.

Royalist as Governor and dubbed Virginia his "Old Dominion" in token of its loyalty. Berkeley welcomed to Virginia a number of Royalist immigrants, called Cavaliers, who strengthened the emerging planter class and whose romantic legend became an important part of Virginia's folklore.

Berkeley's second tenure as Governor was less successful than his first. It ended in a crisis which was the first forewarning of Virginia's resistance to colonial misgovernment. Absorbed in the problems and pleasures of the capital, Berkeley lost touch with the increasing movement of settlers to the west and south of Tidewater Virginia. Perhaps his recent marriage to young Lady Frances Culpeper worsened his temper.

Two miles from Jamestown Governor Berkeley built Green Spring, his home from 1645 until he left Virginia 30 years later. *The Jamestown Foundation*

Perhaps he immersed himself too deeply in his own affairs at Green Spring, his plantation two miles from Jamestown.

Whatever the cause, the Governor failed to protect Virginia's western subjects against the Indians and brought on a rebellion under Nathaniel Bacon, a well-educated young planter. In the ensuing contest Bacon's followers burned Jamestown and demonstrated to King Charles II that his subjects in the New World would accept despotic rule no more readily than would Englishmen along the Thames. The year was 1676 — a hundred years before the Revolution.

As the ablest Governor since Yeardley, Berkeley gave Virginia the stamp of his vibrant personality. Here was the most versatile scholar-statesman of early America — a man of the stripe of William Byrd II and

Governor Alexander Spotswood to come. Though he had narrow social views and mistrusted democracy ("I thank God there are no free schools nor printing, and I hope we shall not have these hundred years," he boasted), Berkeley's net contribution was great. He instilled in the new planter class in Virginia the ideals of English country life, which called for breadth of knowledge and responsibility for the less fortunate. He entertained lavishly, read widely, wrote learnedly, and lived and governed in kingly style. As an erstwhile courtier of Charles I, he had an urbanity which drew to him the leading men of Virginia.

Berkeley's circle at Green Spring was the beginning of a native-born Virginia leadership which in the next 200 years was to push the frontiers of English civilization through southeastern North America. Serving on his Council, in the House of Burgesses, on county courts, and on parish vestries, these men gained experience which was to serve the American colonies in the approaching American Revolution and in the establishment of an independent nation. To these squires, racing English horses or discussing news from London at Green Spring, the example of Berkeley's experimental crops and industries was a valuable one. His home, which his wife described as "the finest seat in America and the only tolerable place for a Governor," was the first mansion in the American wilderness of 1650.

After Bacon's uprising and Berkeley's resignation and return to England, British officials tried again to have their legislation adopted in Virginia and to exercise veto power over the Burgesses' bills. However, the rising resistance of Parliament to monarchical power and the increasing strength of the colonists' will enabled Virginia to resist it. By the time the fourth State House at Jamestown burned in 1698 and the Assembly had voted to move to higher ground, the Virginia House of Burgesses had established its exclusive right to tax Virginia's 70,000 colonists. The period of tutelage under Great Britain's Parliament was ending. A time of growth in the new English nation was about to begin.

The aging Berkeley was threatened in 1676 in the rebellion led by Nathaniel Bacon. *The Mansell Collection, London*

Brick house at Jamestown dating from the 1650 period, reconstructed on basis of archaeological evidence. Designed by A. Lawrence Kocker, Chief Architect Emeritus of Colonial Williamsburg and painted 1957 by Sidney King. *National Park Service*

Modern rendering of the Fourth State House of Jamestown. When it was burned in 1698 the Virginia Assembly moved the capital to Williamsburg, seven miles away. *Life Insurance Co. of Virginia*

5   An Empire in a Wilderness

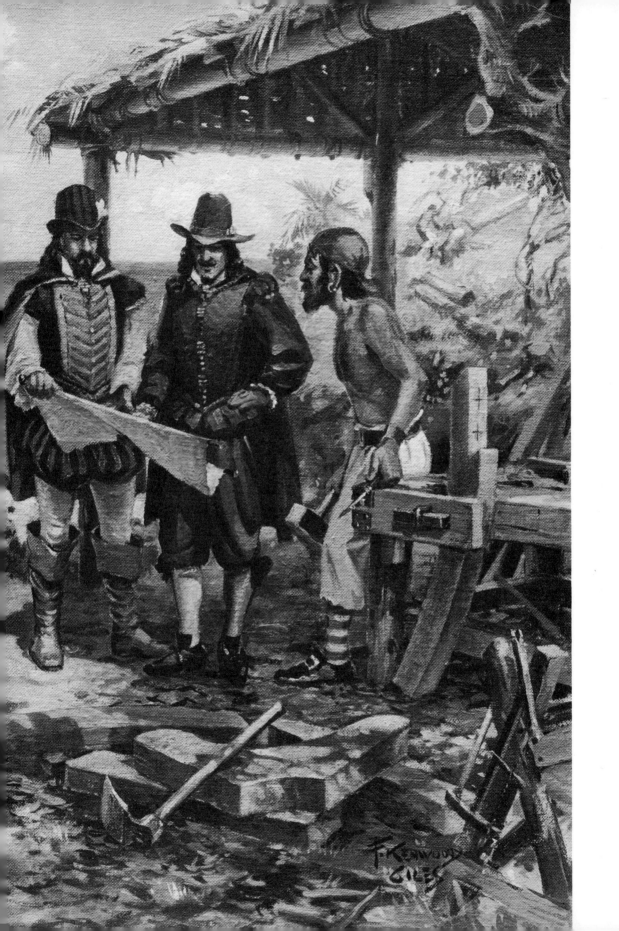

OVERLEAF: When the *Sea Venture*, flagship of Admiral Sir George Somers, foundered on a Bermuda reef in 1609, Governor Sir Thomas Gates and the Admiral had their men build the *Deliverance*, using part of the wreck, and the *Patience*. Two men were left to occupy the islands for England as part of the Virginia claim. *Bermuda News Bureau*

5

THE BRIGHTEST STAR IN ENGLAND'S CROWN: *Jamestown inspires other successful English colonization: Bermuda in 1609; Massachusetts in 1620; New Hampshire in 1623; Maryland in 1634; Rhode Island and Connecticut in 1636. So vast is Virginia's territory that Governor Berkeley in 1641-53 sends expeditions into the West to confirm Virginia's claim to the Ohio Valley and open trade routes. Migration from Virginia helps build up the colonies of North and South Carolina, Georgia, and Alabama. Virginia soldiers like George Washington and explorers like Jim Bridger and Daniel Boone help develop the Ohio Valley.*

An Empire in a Wilderness

The settlement in Virginia stimulated claims to the New World by France as well as by another sea-girt nation which hungered like England for wealth and power: the Netherlands. Here was a nation of merchants and traders who, like the English, were hungry for raw materials from the New World and plunder from Spain. However, the Dutch lacked the foresight of English colonizers. For many years they were content to trade without troubling to establish colonies to give them a permanent foothold in the New World. Belatedly recognizing the advantages of empire, the Netherlands by 1650 became England's chief maritime rival as Spain had been fifty years earlier.

Jealous of England's valuable tobacco trade with Virginia, a fleet of six Dutch ships sailed into the James River in 1667 and burned the English frigate Elizabeth and five merchantmen loaded with tobacco at Newport News. After capturing thirteen other British cargo vessels, the Dutch sailed away.

The shipment of salt from Venezuela had first brought Dutch ships in force to the New World. On their return voyage they brought Dutch manufactures to trade for hides, sugar, tobacco, and pearls with the natives of the Caribbean and South Atlantic areas. From this beginning, Dutch trade with the New World grew rapidly after 1600. The Dutch preyed especially on

t' Fort nieuw Amsterdam op de Manhatans

In 1624 the Dutch defied English claims to North Virginia and placed a colony at the mouth of the Hudson River to traffic in beaver skins. They called it New Amsterdam. *Colonial Williamsburg*

Spanish ships and colonies, for the lowland nation was militantly Protestant and had clashed with Roman Catholic Spain since the Reformation.

Dutch captains also took delight in selling natives from Spain's colonies as slaves in Europe. One of them in 1619 introduced the nefarious trade to Virginia with the delivery of 20 Negroes to Jamestown. Quick to see opportunity for profit, Dutch traders developed a triangular trade between Europe, the Caribbean, and the English colonies in North America. They freighted Dutch manufactures across the Atlantic to the Indies, traded them for sugar and slaves, and brought the latter to Virginia and the other English colonies for tobacco and other products in demand by Europeans.

Tardily realizing the advantage of holding colonies, the Netherlands created a West Indian Company which between 1630 and 1640 settled the islands of Curacao, San Saba, St. Martin, and St. Eustatius in the West Indies. In 1624 the Dutch defied English claims to North Virginia and French settlement in nearby Nova Scotia and placed a colony at the mouth of the Hudson River to begin a traffic in beaver skins.

The most ambitious Dutch achievement was to seize Brazil and the Portuguese slaving stations in West Africa and thus to control Brazilian sugar plantations and their sources of slave labor. Portugal later recovered them, but Dutch aggression in the Caribbean had served the purpose of immobilizing Spain at a crucial time in New World development and of enabling the English to colonize the Atlantic Coast without Spanish opposition, from Newfoundland to Georgia.

From the Dutch, England learned many things that helped her build the greatest empire in the modern world. Alert Dutch shippers opened up trade to many little known islands of the New World. The Protestant bond between the Netherlands and Great Britain allied them in opposition to the colonial ambitions of the Roman Catholic powers. In a sense, Great Britain and the Netherlands became the Spain and the Portugal of the 17th century sea lanes, though there was bitter rivalry between the two.

France also became a threat to English colonization in the New World. A year after Jamestown's settlement, French pioneers under Samuel de Champlain founded the colony of Quebec to trade with Indians for furs. A French colony also took root at Port Royal, Nova Scotia, in 1605, and had become self-supporting when Governor Dale in 1614 sent an expedition from Jamestown, under Samuel Argall, and uprooted it. Argall also destroyed another French settlement at Mount Desert, on the coast of Maine, as an encroachment on England's claims to Virginia.

England's further colonization of the New World now began to move forward. As a consequence of the sinking of the supply ship *Sea Venture* at Bermuda in 1609, while en route to Jamestown with Governor Sir Thomas Gates and other passengers, Bermuda was added to the Virginia claim in 1612. After the survivors had built two new ships, the *Deliverance* and the *Patience*, to take them on to Virginia, several members of the company remained on Bermuda and established an English claim by right of occupancy. On the island Gates left a cross and tablet, reading:

In memory of our deliverance both from the Storm and the Great Leak, we have erected this cross to the honor of God. It is the spoil of an English Ship of 300 tons called "SEA VENTURE," bound with seven others (from which the storm divided us) to Virginia or NOVA BRITANIA in America. In it were two Knights, Sir Thomas Gates, Knight Governor of the English Forces and Colony there;

and Sir George Somers, Knight Admiral of the Seas. Her Captain was Christopher Newport. Passengers and Mariners she had beside (which all come to safety) one hundred and fifty. We were forced to run her ashore (by reason of her leak) under a point that bore South East from the Northern Point of the Island, which we discovered first on the eighth and 20th of July, 1609.

Confirming Gates' claim to Bermuda in Virginia's name, the Virginia Company had its territories extended in the Third Charter of 1612 to include "all islands in the ocean within 300 leagues of Virginia." Attempted British landings a few years later on the islands of Dominica and St. Lucia were beaten off by the native Carib Indians, but English and French settlers jointly occupied St. Kitts, and the English in 1624 settled Barbados, which proved a profitable producer of sugar for the British market. By 1660 its exports briefly exceeded Virginia's in value, entitling Barbados to be called "the brightest jewel in His Majesty's crown."

The attempted settlement of North Virginia, as New England was then designated, met with a reversal for the Plymouth Company a few months after Jamestown was established. An expedition of the Plymouth Company which landed in August, 1607, at the mouth of the Kennebec River, in the present state of Maine, returned in defeat the following spring. For 12 years the Plymouth Company's investors kept hope alive with fishing and trading expeditions. It was on one of these that Captain John Smith, now recovered from the gunpowder wounds he suffered in 1609 at Jamestown, charted the region and called it New England in the same spirit that had led the Spanish to speak of their Caribbean holdings as New Spain and the French to call their American empire New France.

Settlement of New England by the English was finally achieved in 1620 with the landing of the Pilgrims at Plymouth. It was reinforced ten years later by a larger migration of evangelical Anglicans, called Puritans, to Massachusetts Bay. Thus the English served notice that they intended to hold North Virginia against French and Dutch aspirations, just as they had warned Spain earlier by means of the English outpost at Jamestown.

Like Virginia on the lower coast, the Massachusetts Bay Colony became the pivotal English settlement in the north, producing offshoots which were chartered as Connecticut in 1662, Rhode Island in 1663, and New Hampshire in 1679. The pious Pilgrims and Puritans differed in many ways from the more happy-go-lucky Virginians, but Virginia and Massachusetts had much in common. They were to share the leadership of English America until well after the Revolution.

To hold the area of the Atlantic coast that she had claimed as Virginia, England now needed further settlement. Other nations were beginning to covet the area, and some had planted colonists there. To secure the upper Chesapeake Bay, King Charles I of England chartered the colony of Maryland in 1632. Thirty-two years later the English took over the Dutch colony of New Amsterdam and renamed it New York. The remaining coastal area became New Jersey and Delaware. The first inland colony was chartered in 1681 when the Crown granted Pennsylvania to William Penn and his followers.

South of Virginia, where Spain remained a latent threat, King Charles II made a grant in 1665 of part of the London Company's original Virginia claim. Named in honor of King Charles, it was ultimately divided into the colonies of North and South Carolina. Even farther south the Brit-

Governor Sir Thomas Dale sent expeditions from Jamestown under Captain Samuel Argall which wiped out French settlements on Mount Desert, Maine, and Port Royal, Nova Scotia. *Central Office of Information, London*

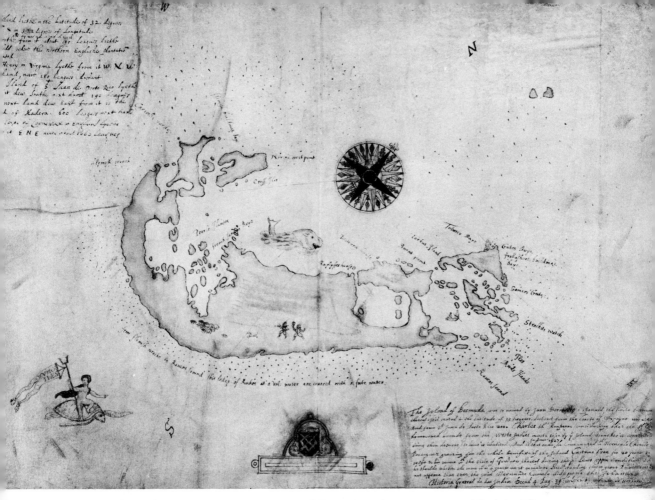

Admiral Sir George Somers drew a map of Bermuda while en route to Virginia. The islands for years after his shipwreck there were called the Somers or Summer Isles.

ish in 1732 dared to establish the colony of Georgia, encouraged by the fact that the Spanish settlement planted at St. Augustine in 1565 had not attempted to push northward.

Thus England within 125 years of the settlement at Jamestown held 13 colonies shoulder-to-shoulder along the Atlantic coast.

The territory designated originally as Virginia was largest, for most of the other colonies except Pennsylvania were bounded on the west by the Appalachian mountain range, which roughly paralleled the Atlantic coast a few hundred miles inland. Vir-

ginia, by contrast, extended northwesterly across the continent to the unknown sea beyond. Even after the British had ceded their claim and Virginia's to territory west of the Mississippi River in 1763, Virginia held title to the extensive Northwest Territory, her upper boundary following the course of the Great Lakes. By means of this gerrymander, the Virginia Company in its charter of 1609 had hoped to include the presumed water route through the continent to the western sea.

During England's colonization of North America, the course of settlement was constantly westward. Virginia, with much to gain, led this effort. She began it when Captain Christopher Newport in 1607 explored the James River as far west as the falls at the present site of Richmond. John Smith continued it in explorations of Virginia's rivers aboard the pinnace *Discovery* until he returned to England in 1610. Smith sent a hearsay report to Henry Hudson of "a sea leading into the western ocean, by the north of the southern English colony," and Indians vaguely confirmed the report. However, exploration for a time was balked at the fall-line along the foothills of the Appalachian Range, which created a coastal shelf from the Gaspé Peninsula in Canada southward almost to the Gulf of Mexico.

An effort to penetrate the continent to the west of the Appalachians was made by Sir William Berkeley after he became Governor in 1642. Fur traders at the fall lines of Virginia's rivers were encountering difficulties with Indian middlemen, and they petitioned the General Assembly for permission to explore further. Following the massacre of 1644, the Governor and the Assembly ordered forts set up along six Virginia rivers to serve as bases for further exploration.

Typical of these was Fort Henry, which was built by Abraham Wood in 1646 near the mouth of the Appomattox River, on the present site of Petersburg. Once he had built it, Wood led a party of three fellow explorers, two servants, and a guide on horseback into what are now Kentucky and Tennessee, over the 1,500-mile Virginia Traders' Path. They hoped to verify an Indian account that "within five days' jour-

British settlement of the West Indies began on the islands of St. Kitts and Barbados. A contemporary print shows an English plantation. *Thomas L. Williams*

To secure the upper Chesapeake Bay area and deter European settlement on the Atlantic coast, King Charles I of England chartered Maryland in 1632 under Lord Calvert. *Maryland Dept. of Economic Development*

ney to the westward and by south, there is a great high mountain, and at the foot thereof, great rivers that run into a great sea; and that there are men that come thither in ships . . . and have reed caps on their heads, and ride on beasts like our horses, but have much longer ears." This was interpreted to mean that the Gulf of Mexico, which De-Soto was known to have explored, lay only ten days' journey away. Wood's journey brought no such reward, but it advanced the settlement of the region beyond the Appalachians.

When Berkeley resumed the governorship for the second time in 1661, after the Cromwells' rule, he became King Charles II's principal policy agent in the American colonies. Recognizing England's interest in the unexplored lands beyond the mountains, he asked the King in 1668 for permission to send an expedition westward. The King was financially involved and declined, but Berkeley sent the German physician John Lederer on three expeditions in 1669, and 1670, which scaled the Blue Ridge and Appalachian ranges, searching for passes through which traders and settlers might penetrate the mountains to the west.

Abraham Wood renewed his efforts in 1671 by sending four explorers west "for the finding out the ebbing and flowing of the waters on the other side of the mountains in order to the discovery of the South Sea." The group inched through the forest for 16 days and reached a tributary of the Mississippi River before being forced back. They reported to Wood, "We first proclaimed the King in these words: 'Long live Charles the Second, by the grace of God, King of England, Scotland, France, Ireland, and Virginia.'" Then they fired a salute and carved four trees with marks for Charles II, Governor Berkeley, Wood, and their Indian guide, Perecute.

Another group sent southwest by Wood in 1673 followed the Occoneechee Indian trail to find where the Blue Ridge Mountains ended. After 15 days of rugged riding, they came to a Cherokee town at the headwaters of the Tennessee River. One explorer was murdered by an Occoneechee guide, and the other narrowly missed being burned at the stake by the Cherokees.

Wood was the earliest and most persistent of Virginia's explorers. He had come from England as an indentured servant, and like many others had worked his way to freedom and the ownership of land. Another early explorer was William Byrd I, son of a London goldsmith and heir through his uncle to valuable Virginia lands. From his estate, Belvidire, on the present site of Richmond, and later from Westover on the James, Byrd loaded caravans of a hundred or more horses with European goods and sent them west to trade with the Indians for furs.

The most effective promoter of trade and exploration in Virginia's second century was Governor Alexander Spotswood. Governing from 1710 to 1722, he directed his efforts to expanding Virginia's frontiers,

keeping peace with the Indians, and establishing tribal settlements to prevent the Indians' extermination. Spotswood's most famous exploit was to lead a group of horsemen from Williamsburg in 1716 to the top of the Blue Ridge Mountains, with the aid of servants and abundant food and drink. The exploit kindled interest in westward migration. It also gained imperishable renown for the jewelled golden horseshoes that Spotswood gave his riders.

What *did* lie west of Virginia? The question continued to pique Virginians. It remained for the most curious of them all to learn the answer. In 1792 Thomas Jefferson began a subscription among members of the American Philosophical Society, in Philadelphia, to send the botanist Andre Michaux to explore the northwest "by ascending the Missouri, crossing the Stony [Rocky] Mountains, and descending the nearest river to the Pacific." Jefferson observed that "It would seem from the latest maps as if a

Governor Alexander Spotswood pushed Virginia westward from 1710 to 1722 and led his "Knights of the Golden Horseshoe" from Williamsburg to the mountains. *The Valentine Museum*

William Byrd I sent pack trains of 100 horses from the James River into the southwestern Virginia mountains to trade with the Indians for furs to be shipped to England. *Virginia State Library*

river called Oregon [Columbia], interlocked with the Missouri for a considerable distance, and entered the Pacific Ocean."

The exploration was made at last by Meriwether Lewis and William Clark, both of Virginia, in 1805-6. It was the most important continental exploration ever undertaken in America, leading to acquisition by the United States of the vital Pacific northwest. After 200 years of speculation, it proved that the transcontinental water route did not exist.

Despite exploration and the fur trade, the undeveloped majority of Virginia west of the Appalachians was to remain virtually unknown to Virginians until the French began moving into the Ohio Valley about 1748 as a means of linking their early possessions in Canada with newer claims in the Illinois country and in Louisiana. France's object has been described as "joining hands behind the backs" of the English colonies, which stood shoulder-to-shoulder along the Atlantic. To counter French strategy, Virginia granted a large tract in the Ohio Valley in 1749 to a group of land speculators. France retaliated by sending an expedition to the Ohio to claim the area and build three forts.

To these forts Virginia in 1753 sent a protest against French occupation. It was carried by a 21-year-old soldier who had already seen hard service on the Virginia frontier. This was the first important mission to be entrusted to George Washington, but it was only the beginning of a career unmatched in American history. When the French refused to accept Virginia's protest, Lieutenant Governor Robert Dinwiddie dispatched the Virginia militia to hold the site of Pittsburgh, at the juncture of the Allegheny and Monongahela rivers. Virginia militia under Washington successfully fought the French at Fort Duquesne, and regular troops were brought over from France and England to join the fray.

The 21-year-old George Washington in 1753 was sent by Virginia to the Ohio Valley to protest French occupation of the colony's territory. *Washington and Lee University*

Virginia's early claims to the Pacific were not fully explored until Meriwether Lewis and William Clark ranged from St. Louis westward to Oregon in 1805-6. *Thomas L. Williams*

The ensuing French and Indian War, spreading from the New World to the Old, was bitterly fought for seven years before British forces captured Quebec and Montreal and achieved a peace favorable to England. France yielded her claim to all North American territory east of the Mississippi River except two islands in the Gulf of St. Lawrence. By this peace the English ceded the claims that Virginia made to lands west of the Mississippi under her charter of 1609, but the Old Dominion could continue to claim a wide swath of undeveloped land east of the Mississippi, from the Appalachians northward to the Great Lakes. By the same treaty, Spain, which had joined the war in Europe against England, ceded Florida to England.

Until the French invaded the Ohio Valley in mid-century, the English colonies in America had acted largely independently of each other. Direction came to each from England, and they had no occasion to work together except when menaced. Such was their aloofness that when a congress of colonies gathered in 1754 at Albany to deal with the French in the Ohio Valley, Virginia sent no delegates for lack of funds. Furthermore, the eight colonies which sent representatives rejected as unnecessary a plan drawn up by Benjamin Franklin, of Pennsylvania, for an intercolonial council on defense and Indian control.

Now, in retrospect, the colonies realized that the French and Indian War showed need for concerted policy in British America against European aggression. At last they were becoming conscious of common interests. It was only a short step to united action against England herself. In this movement Virginia was to lead.

6 The World That Revolved Around Williamsburg

THE WORLD THAT REVOLVED AROUND WILLIAMSBURG: *The capital of Virginia is moved from Jamestown to Williamsburg in 1699. The College of William and Mary (1693) becomes a training ground for leaders, including Thomas Jefferson, James Monroe, John Marshall. The plantation system develops a country gentry trained in law, agriculture and local administration, who are indispensable when the American Revolution comes. Great minds speak up in debate in the legislative assembly at Williamsburg which hears the voices of George Mason, Richard Henry Lee, Patrick Henry, George Wythe, Edmund Pendleton, George Washington. Williamsburg produces Peyton Randolph, who is to become the first president of the Continental Congress; Edmund Randolph, who proposes a bicameral federal legislature, and Richard Bland, who advocates a ring of self-governing British colonies, united by loyalty to the Crown.*

6

The World That Revolved Around Williamsburg

On October 31, 1698, the fourth State House accidentally burned to the ground at Jamestown. In disgust, the Virginia General Assembly voted to move Virginia's capital from the marshy peninsula on the James to Middle Plantation six miles inland. The Assembly renamed the village Williamsburg in honor of King William III, who had succeeded King James I's grandson, James II, as King. While a capitol was being constructed, the legislators met in the newly built college. Jamestown declined. Brick from the burned capital were hauled by wagon to build the new town.

Jamestown soon gave way to Williamsburg as the center of Virginia life. Located midway between the James and the York rivers, it was accessible to ocean-going sailing ships by a deep creek from each. In 1693, when it was no more than a crossroads village, it had been designated by the Assembly as the site for the College of William and Mary, the first institution of higher learning in the colonies since Harvard College was founded in 1636. When it was opened several years later, learned clerics came from Great Britain to teach there. For the first time Virginia could train

men for the church, for public service, and for teaching without sending them to Oxford, Cambridge, or Edinburgh. Clergymen were especially needed, for many parishes lacked churches.

The rapid development of leadership in the colony in the eighteenth century was due largely to the presence of the college and the leadership of its president, the Reverend James Blair. Educated at the University of Edinburgh and ordained in the Church of England, this strong-willed Scotsman arrived in 1685 in Henrico County, near the present Richmond, as a missionary. Four years later he was named by the Bishop of London, who was responsible for the Anglican Church in the American colonies, as his deputy, or commissary, in Virginia.

The Reverend James Blair, deputy of the Bishop of London in Virginia, obtained royal approval for a college and became its president for life. *Colonial Williamsburg*

Blair soon made his bishop aware of Virginia's tremendous needs, which had accumulated during the eighty-two years in which Virginia's spiritual affairs had been directed from London. When the General Assembly in 1691 voted to establish a college, it sent Blair to England to present its request.

Petitioning the King's representatives in London, Blair pointed out that "Virginians have souls to save as well as Englishmen." "Souls?" the King's Attorney-General exploded. "Damn your souls! Make tobacco!" With the help of Blair's fellow clergymen, King William and Queen Mary were persuaded in 1693 to grant the charter, and he returned to Virginia and was named president of the college for life. In 1964 he accepted additional charge of the church at Jamestown, which remained the colony's "court church" so long as the capital remained there. After the seat of government was moved to Williamsburg in 1699, Blair became rector of Bruton Parish there.

Energetic and single-minded James Blair worked for the Christian faith and education all his life. In his fifty years as president of William and Mary, he fought off attempts of one governor after another to dominate it. In the tight bureaucracy of Williamsburg, the Governor and the Commissary were the two controlling figures. It is not surprising that they clashed. Gover-

The College of William and Mary was the temporary meeting place of the Virginia Assembly from 1700 to 1705, when the Capitol in Williamsburg was erected. The central building is in the style of Christopher Wren. Flanking it were Brafferton Hall, intended for the education of the Indians, and the President's House. *Colonial Williamsburg*

nors Sir Edmund Andros and Colonel Francis Nicholson, both originally supporters of the college, became its foes after colliding with Blair. Governor Spotswood, the ablest Virginia governor in the eighteenth century, was recalled like his predecessors through the influence of the Commissary.

Creation of the college and the strengthening of the church filled so great a need in Virginia that Blair made himself one of the key figures in the colony's growth. He conceived himself to be Virginia's preceptor, and he was. Like the political churchmen of the Middle Ages, his influence penetrated all areas of life. He was the Bishop's deputy, a minister, teacher, and powerful member of the Council of State from 1694 until 1743. He was Virginia's "Lord High Everything Else."

While Blair succeeded in his effort to provide Virginia with a college, he was less successful in strengthening the Church. He was unable to increase the numbers or the influence of the clergy, who had suffered from long years of absentee administration by the unconcerned Bishop of London. Not even a standing offer of the board of visitors of William and Mary to provide 50 pounds to send any divinity student to England for ordination drew candidates for the ministry.

The chief service of the new college was to train the ablest of the colonies' young men to take over the government of English America. Before William and Mary had opened its doors, higher education was possible only for the few Virginians who crossed the Atlantic to study at universities. While plantation life had produced many men of breadth and judgment, Virginia in its first century had paid scant attention to scholarship, literature, philosophy, theology, or the arts. The new college from the moment of its opening now stimulated these.

By the time of James Blair's death in 1743, William and Mary had nearly fifty students, taught by half a dozen masters, in its college. An unknown number of younger men attended its preparatory grammar school. It had not grown as fast as Harvard College, which in the same year had 104 undergraduates, or Yale, founded at New Haven in 1701, which had 78. However, the calibre of its instruction and its students was clearly evident in the leadership which was developing in eighteenth century Virginia. "I know of no place in the world, while the present professors remain, where I would so soon place a son," wrote Thomas Jefferson, one of its graduates, later.

As capital of Virginia, Williamsburg

The World That Revolved Around Williamsburg [103]

soon grew into Virginia's chief village. Its winding main road, which was part of the trail which had linked Fort Algernon to Jamestown, was straightened, and a town plan was drawn by Governor Francis Nicholson. He named the 99-foot central avenue for the Duke of Gloucester, infant heir to the throne, and placed the Capitol at the eastern end, facing the college. Halfway down this mile-long street stood Bruton Parish Church, a small brick church built about 1674 and replaced in 1715 by a larger structure, more appropriate to the dignity of the Governor and the Assembly. Bisecting the principal thoroughfare was a greensward leading to the mansion built for the Governor, known as "The Palace" because of its grandeur and expense.

Under Nicholson's plan for a "green country town," Williamsburg was divided into half-acre lots on which dwellings were set back by law six feet from the street for uniformity. The Italian Renaissance plan

The first Bruton Parish Church, built about 1674 near the crossroads of Middle Plantation. *The Jamestown Foundation*

was a far cry from Jamestown's shapeless row housing. It offered both better ventilation, sanitation, and defense against fire. On its rectangular plots colonial officials formerly at Jamestown built clapboard and brick houses copied from British builders' manuals. Intermingled along Duke of Gloucester Street were the shops and homes of lawyers, tradesmen, and innkeepers. Taverns increased, for during Public Times

A century after Jamestown was settled Virginia had become prosperous from the export of tobacco, grown on plantations worked by slaves. *The Arents Collection, New York Public Library*

Williamsburg drew visitors in the latter eighteenth century from not only the present Virginia but from settlements in what are now West Virginia and Kentucky.

The men who came to make the colony's laws in Virginia's second century were far different from those who had settled James-town. By 1707 Virginia had begun to acquire the gloss of wealth, thanks to its tobacco economy. Descendants of the surviving pioneers were building homes like those of English gentlemen. They dressed in the fashion of London. Plantation life was preparing them for self-government,

The World That Revolved Around Williamsburg [105]

The rebuilt Capitol of Virginia as it stands today in Colonial Williamsburg, testifying to the solidity, architectural taste and prosperity of the eighteenth-century colony. *Colonial Williamsburg*

for it required knowledge, judgment, and a concern for the ignorant and defenseless slaves.

The wrong of slavery was not yet apparent to most Virginians, for they had come from the Old World at a time of inherited class distinctions, and they accepted differences in men's lot as God's will. Besides, slavery offered cheap labor for tobacco culture, which brought Virginia wealth. A new and more enlightened age, enriched by the Christian humanism of John Locke and the French Enlightenment, was beginning to emerge, but change comes slowly in the rural world.

The founding of William and Mary revealed the need for more grammar schools to prepare youths to train for the profession. While parents and a few tutors taught children of planter families to read, write, and do sums, few boys and fewer girls went on to the handfull of colonial grammar schools, most of them conducted by ministers like the Reverend James Maury, who taught Jefferson. Until the onset of the Revolution, some families sent sons to English public schools. Most young people learned only as much as their parents could teach them. A few free schools were set up, the first in Hampton in 1634-35 by gift of Benjamin Syms. The education of slaves was neglected except by a few plantation owners and clergymen.

Educated men, except clergy, were expected to serve on parish vestries and in higher offices. From county office it was only a step upward to the House of Burgesses. The Council of State, nominated by the Governor and appointed by the King, was the highest rank in this loose but effective aristocracy of wealth, education, and ability. Membership on the Council was

A sketch of the Capitol where the House of Burgesses met. *Colonial Williamsburg*

highly valued and over the years came to be an almost hereditary privilege of powerful Tidewater families. It was, in a sense, Virginia's House of Lords.

During the annual session of the General Assembly and General Court, Williamsburg was crowded with Burgesses to make laws for His Majesty's oldest and largest colony. Patrick Henry could be heard haranguing the Burgesses in words charged with electric eloquence. George Washington might

The Governor's House, known as the Palace, the most elaborately furnished of the official buildings. *Colonial Williamsburg*

The World That Revolved Around Williamsburg   [107]

Patrick Henry of Hanover County, the boldest critic of English administration among the Burgesses. From a painting. *Colonial Williamsburg*

be seen at prayer in Bruton Parish Church. Had you been a close friend of the Governor's, you might hear the student Thomas Jefferson play his violin at a gathering in the Palace. Such was Williamsburg in those years.

The part Virginians played in making their laws, begun at Jamestown in 1619, increased as they gradually overcame the basic needs of feeding and clothing themselves, controlling the Indians, and protecting their frontiers. As they did so, they differed increasingly with England in economic and political matters. The liberalism of Rousseau and the Enlightenment, coupled with that of John Locke, found friendly soil at William and Mary, which stimulated a new generation with talk of liberty, fraternity, and equality. Despite its administration by the Church of England, the Deism of French philosophers took root

there. Democratic frontier legislators who came by horse to represent western Virginia in the Assembly added to the ferment of ideas.

In this vital era, future leaders of the Revolution learned how to make and enforce the law. In its years as capital, from 1699 to 1779, Williamsburg became a living part of America's growth toward self-government, its respect for human dignity, and its belief in individual rights and responsibilities. The eighteenth century was in a sense a germination of seeds sown at Jamestown toward a harvest to be reaped at Yorktown.

In the Virginia capital of less than 2,000 people lived many men who would leave their mark on history. In Williamsburg lived Richard Bland, who in his *An Enquiry Into the Rights of the British Colonies*, published in 1766, first proposed a British commonwealth of nations, linked to the mother country through loyalty to the Crown. There the lawyer George Wythe taught Jefferson and John Marshall and took part in the pre-Revolutionary debates of the Burgesses. There lived St. George Tucker, author of the first American textbook on the law.

From his house on the Courthouse Green, Peyton Randolph could look across Market Square to the home of his nephew, Edmund Randolph; the former would be first President of the Continental Congress in Philadelphia, while the latter would become a pillar of the Constitutional Convention, first Attorney General of the United States, and Secretary of State under George Washington. Also in Williamsburg lived Cyrus Griffin, who was president of the last Continental Congress and judge of the United States Court of Appeals; Littleton

An unusual group of able men lived in Williamsburg in the mid-eighteenth century and took part in events leading to the American Revolution. They included (top row, left to right): the learned lawyer and law teacher George Wythe, who signed the Declaration of Independence; St. George Tucker, author of the first American textbook of law, and Edmund Randolph, who presented Virginia's plan to the Constitutional Convention in Philadelphia and became the first Attorney General of the United States. On the lower row, left to right, are Littleton Waller Tazewell, who became Governor and Senator; William Wirt, a native of Maryland who became Monroe's Attorney General, and Cyrus Griffin, who was president of the last Continental Congress. *Portraits of Wythe and Tucker from Colonial Williamsburg, others from Virginia State Library*

Waller Tazewell, who became a renowned lawyer and Governor; and William Wirt, who practiced law in Williamsburg and wrote some of his *The Letters of the British Spy* before becoming Attorney General under Monroe and candidate for President in 1832.

At the Capitol in Williamsburg, Patrick Henry inflamed the colonies with his warning, "Let George III profit by their example." In the same chamber, Edmund Pendleton on May 15, 1776, offered the Virginia *Resolutions for Independence*, which in turn led Richard Henry Lee in Philadelphia to call on the Continental Congress to announce, on July 4, that "These united colonies are, and of right ought to be, free and independent States." There George Mason offered on May 15, 1776, his *Declaration of Rights*, which demanded for Virginians the security of government by law, which was to be incorporated by Madison into the *Bill of Rights* of the *United States Constitution*. George Washington and James Madison began their legislative careers in the same Capitol, while James Monroe and John Tyler were learning their lessons at the college.

Governors Francis Fauquier and Norborne Berkeley, Baron de Botetourt, attempted to mediate between angry Virginia colonists and the Crown, but without success. *Virginia Historical Society*

Associated with the colonials were a number of exceptional men who came from England to serve as Governor, as president of the college, or in other roles. Among them were the Rev. Hugh Jones, professor of mathematics and natural philosophy at William and Mary, who wrote a useful book about Virginia and produced the first English grammar in the colonies. Dr. William Small, professor of natural philosophy and mathematics, was Jefferson's favorite teacher and developed his interest in science. The Welsh poet, Goronway Owen, came to teach in the college and serve the Church in Virginia as a minister.

Many of the governors were men of unusual attainments, though most of their efforts to influence British policy as the century wore on were thwarted by the policies of King George III and his ministers. Francis Nicholson did much to advance the College. Alexander Spotswood encouraged industry. Francis Fauquier talked metaphysics with the student Jefferson. Norborne Berkeley, Baron Botetourt, endeared himself so completely to Virginia that his statue stood unharmed in the Capitol after the Revolution had engulfed Virginia.

Most of William and Mary's early masters were clergymen and Scotsmen, like the Reverend Mungo Inglis, whose appointment drew complaint from Governor Andros that Blair was "filling the colony" with his Scottish countrymen. (Despite the union of England and Scotland under James I, the colony regarded itself as English.) Virginia was indeed changing, and not only Scots but Irish, Welsh, French, and Germans came in with the change.

The Scots came first as clergymen-scholars and then as merchants in the ports of York, Hampton, Norfolk, Portsmouth, Falmouth, Suffolk, Alexandria, Port Royal, Smithfield, Petersburg, and Richmond. Shrewd and Tory in their politics, they were first disdained by the English, who looked on Tory traders with the same suspicion as had Sir Edwin Sandys a hundred years before. However, the merchants and traders were too necessary to be ignored. From their thrift they grew rich, giving them a position which permitted their children to intermarry with planter families. When the Revolution came, most of them were so much a part of Virginia that they stayed and fought as Revolutionaries. Their descendants exercised increasing influence in Virginia.

Settlement of seventeenth century Virginia spread upriver along the James, the York, the Rappahannock, and the Potomac Rivers only as far as the fall line, which provided a barrier against water transport of tobacco. However, this barrier was hurdled in the year 1700 when 200 French Huguenot refugees were permitted by Virginia's government to settle on 10,000 acres of land on the south shore of the James some 20 miles upriver from the fall-line village which was to become Richmond.

Within a year, 800 of these French Protestants were farming at or near Manakin Town, the abandoned site of a Monacan Indian village. Their leader, Benjamin de Joux, had been ordained an Anglican minister, and they were readily assimilated into Virginia's agrarian and Protestant life. As they prospered, many moved upriver to new lands, losing national identity and language through intermarriage with the English. Today little more than their family names, such as Michaux, Duvall, Moncure, and Munford, remind Virginians of these hard-working pioneers.

Early Virginia leaders for independence were Edmund Pendleton of Caroline County, who offered the Virginia Resolutions on May 15, 1776; Richard Henry Lee of Westmoreland County, who presented the Resolutions to the Continental Congress, and George Mason of Gunston Hall in Fairfax County, whose Virginia Declaration of Rights was adopted the same year. *Colonial Williamsburg*

Yorktown, on the York River near Williamsburg, became a leading tobacco port. *The Mariners Museum*

To encourage settlement in the rolling foothills which lay between the Tidewater plain and the western mountains, the colony made large grants of land in the 1730s and 1740s. It also agreed to open up lands in the Valley of Virginia to streams of Scotch-Irish and Germans who were migrating south from Pennsylvania in search of farm and grazing lands. The rugged and rocky Valley was less fertile than the Tidewater plain, but the emigrants found it a beautiful homeland, reminiscent of the Scottish Highlands. There they cleared and worked farms with their own hands, finding slavery both morally objectionable and unsuited to their needs.

The Scotch-Irish were permitted to worship as Presbyterians, for the Act of Union which linked England and Scotland designated the Church of Scotland as the Established Church in that country. They set up well-taught academies in the Valley of Virginia which drew students from a wide area to prepare for the College of William and Mary and the Presbyterian college, Nassau Hall, at Princeton, New Jersey. One academy, founded by John Brown near Staunton in Augusta County in 1749, was to become Washington and Lee University. Another, founded in Prince Edward County in 1775, became Hampden-Sydney College the next year.

By 1749 the frontier of Virginia had moved upward from the fall line of its river to the crest of the Blue Ridge and thence across the Valley to the crest of the Alleghanies. Because it was easier to penetrate rivers than forests, colonists had pushed their way upland along the James, the Roanoke, the Rappahannock, the Potomac, and the Shenandoah. This movement had peopled the Valley with a mixture of English, Scotch-Irish, Germans, and Huguenots representing old and new Virginia. The tide of settlers now confronted the vast Indian area of Virginia which lay to the southwest — the territory which was to become Kentucky and West Virginia.

Already it was difficult for the capital at Williamsburg to keep up with its spreading colonists, west of the Blue Ridge. Virginia was growing into an empire.

Presbyterians in the Virginia upcountry founded many academies, including Prince Edward Academy in 1775. It became Hampden-Sydney College the next year. *Hampden-Sydney College*

7   The War That Produced A New Nation

THE WAR THAT PRODUCED A NEW ENGLISH NATION: *Virginia takes a leading part in the French and Indian War and in conquering the Northwest Territory, an empire later given to the United States. Virginia and Massachusetts, as the most mature American colonies, take the lead in America's assertion of independence. Edmund Pendleton offers the Virginia Resolutions for Independence on May 15, 1776, in Williamsburg and the Assembly adopts them and sends them to Philadelphia, where Virginia's Richard Henry Lee in June calls for a declaration of independence. George Washington is chosen commander-in-chief. Ironically, once-loyal Virginia is among the most ardently revolutionist of the colonies, although it stands to lose heavily because of its agrarian dependence on commercial Britain and because its businessmen have relatively few debts that can be repudiated in wartime. The war in its final stages moves to Virginia, and General Cornwallis explains: "I was most firmly persuaded, that, until Virginia was reduced, we could not hold the more southern provinces, and that, after its reduction, they could fall without more difficulty." The crucial battle occurs at Yorktown, only twenty miles from Virginia's first settlement at Jamestown.*

The War That Produced A New Nation

Whether Raleigh envisioned his "new English nation" as a dominion or an independent nation, no one knows. The concept of nationhood in Sir Walter's time was new and uncertain. The poetic knight-adventurer seldom used nouns in their literal sense. Whatever his intent, it was inevitable that settlers amid such vast natural riches as Virginia's would in time gain the desire for independence, especially since they had from the beginning believed themselves due the rights, immunities, and privileges of Englishmen living in England.

On these premises, Virginians could be expected to long for independence whenever their sense of being wronged was sup-

ported by sufficient strength to correct it. And this was the more inevitable because England's powerful commercial interests believed that colonies existed primarily for the financial benefit of the homeland.

Neither mother country nor colony could be entirely blamed for the conflict which developed between them in the eighteenth century. As their interests parted, so did their affection. Nor were the human failings of governors or deputy governors to blame. They were generally able men, and they often sympathized with Virginians in their contests with the Crown. No man could have reconciled the life-and-death concerns of settlers with the long-term ob-

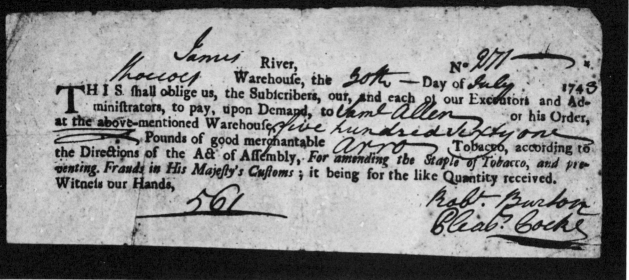

Currency was scarce in plantation Virginia, and tobacco warehouse receipts were used in lieu of money. *College of William and Mary*

jects of British colonial policy, which sought to promote British shipping, manufacturing, and insurance interests by limiting their colonies' production to simple raw materials.

The problem was not limited to Virginia. It had arisen first in Virginia, paradoxically enough, because Virginians were so thoroughly English in their consciousness of their rights. They knew that Magna Carta and the Parliamentary debates of James I and Charles I had affirmed that Parliament, representing the people, was the guardian of British liberty. They knew also that Parliament in the Revolution Settlement of 1688 had taken control from the Crown of the passing of laws, the levying of taxes, and the maintenance of troops. They believed themselves to be as thoroughly British as anyone alive. They had stood up for their rights against Governor Berkeley in Bacon's Rebellion in 1676; against English tobacco-buyers in the General Assembly's protest in the 1730s; and in Virginians' resistance in 1753 to Governor Robert Dinwiddie's attempt to impose a land patent fee of one pistole.

Virginians gained confidence as they gained population and wealth. As early as 1716, Governor Spotswood was complaining of them: "By their professions and actions, they seem to allow no jurisdiction, civil or ecclesiastical, but what is established by laws of their own making." Yet in behaving thus, they were merely doing what Englishmen had won the right to do: to criticize government in an effort to force a reconsideration of policy. Such criticism did not imply disloyalty. In fact, the English parliamentary system had devised channels through which such protests could be heard.

Relations between Great Britain and Virginia were amicable so long as Virginians received good prices for tobacco and felt they were taxed no more harshly than their British kinsmen. The Rev. Hugh Jones of the faculty of the College of William and Mary was one of many visitors who noted Virginia's identification with England. Writing in 1724, he observed that "The habits, life, customs, computations, etc. of the Virginians are much the same as about London,

British mercantile policy in the eighteenth century limited colonies to production of raw materials for Britain's manufacture. Tobacco shipments from Virginia's plantation docks were the main source of income. *Thomas L. Williams*

which they esteem their home." He described the colony as "the most ancient and loyal, the most pleasing and flourishing, the most extensive and beneficial colony belonging to the Crown of Great Britain . . . the happy retreat of true Britons."

This affection for the motherland began to diminish noticeably toward the middle of the eighteenth century in Virginia and the other twelve colonies. One reason was that His Majesty's Government increasingly tried to limit them to the production of raw materials, against their interest and wishes; this policy had been evident as early as 1699, when Parliament forbade Americans to export woolen goods or even to trade them

among themselves. A second cause was legislation which permitted the colonies to ship only in British vessels and to British consignees, eliminating the advantageous "triangular trade" developed by the Dutch. The third and strongest cause was Parliament's ill-considered adoption in 1763 of a series of colonial taxes to refill Crown coffers depleted by Britain's Seven Years' War with France.

Patrick Henry's speech against the Stamp Act in the House of Burgesses in 1765 was the most notable early protest against this program. Henry's resolutions declared that the Virginia Assembly had sole power to tax Virginians. They were adopted enthusi-

The Continental Congress in 1775 chose George Washington Commander-in-Chief of colonial forces in the war with Great Britain. *Colonial Williamsburg*

Virginia signers of the Declaration of Independence were Thomas Nelson Jr., Thomas Jefferson, George Wythe, Carter Braxton, Francis Lightfoot Lee, Benjamin Harrison, and Richard Henry Lee, brother of Francis. *Diorama at Jamestown Festival Park. The Jamestown Foundation*

astically after the Hanover County Burgess had declared: "Caesar had his Brutus; Charles the First his Cromwell; and George the Third . . ." Here Henry was interrupted by cries of "Treason! Treason!" Whereupon he calmly concluded, ". . . may profit by their example."

Virginia's Stamp Act Resolutions were circulated to other colonies, and Massachusetts called an intercolonial congress which met in New York and petitioned King George III and Parliament to rescind the offensive measure. They did, but other affronts were to come.

Burgesses in Virginia kept informed of other colonies' reactions to British tax mea-sures by a Committee of Correspondence, which spread confidential advice on defying them throughout the 13 colonies. The Committee was revived at a secret meeting in Williamsburg in 1773 between Richard Henry Lee, Patrick Henry, Thomas Jefferson, Francis Lightfoot Lee, and Dabney Carr. Later that year Bostonians staged their Tea Party in protest against a new British tax on tea, and Massachusetts was placed under punitive British control. The Virginia Burgesses showed their sympathy with a day of fasting and prayer, beginning with services at Bruton Parish Church. When Governor Lord Dunmore dissolved the Virginia Assembly, the Burgesses met in Ra-

The War That Produced A New Nation [123]

leigh Tavern and issued a call to the twelve other colonies to meet and unite in resistance.

The Continental Congress that resulted in Philadelphia was chiefly the creation of Virginia and Massachusetts. Over the moderate objections of Pennsylvania's John Dickinson, the aroused anger of the two oldest colonies dominated the debates of the Congress. Speaker Peyton Randolph of the Virginia Burgesses was elected presiding officer, and arguments against British policy advanced by Richard Bland and Thomas Jefferson in their pamphlets against British policy were incorporated in its conclusions.

A second Continental Congress met in 1775 after colonists in Massachusetts had battled British troops at Lexington and Concord in the first actual armed conflict of the Revolution. The Congress chose George Washington as its Commander-in-Chief and quietly prepared for a war with Great Britain, which now seemed inescapable.

The Virginia Convention that met in Williamsburg in 1776 set in motion action by the colonial governments which produced the *Declaration of Independence*. On May 15 Speaker Edmund Pendleton submitted to the convention his *Resolutions for Independence*. Adopted unanimously, they were carried by rider to Philadelphia, where Virginia's delegate Richard Henry Lee on June 7 called on the Continental Congress to declare the colonies free. Jefferson then drafted the *Declaration of Independence*, which was formally adopted on July 4. "It is fitting for a Virginian to be at the head of this business," said John Adams in persuading Jefferson to draw up the document.

At the Virginia convention in 1776 George Mason also offered his *Declaration of Rights*, which assured the continuity of

Anglo-Saxon law in America and later inspired the first ten amendments in 1791 to the *United States Constitution*. The spirit of the articles was the spirit of Magna Carta: the inviolability of individual rights against government oppression. The Declaration was adopted and became the model for similar pronouncements in other colonies.

Adoption of the *Declaration of Independence* was the final step toward a war that neither Great Britain nor America could avoid. Too late, Great Britain realized the strength of the colonists' will. In the five years of the war, thousands of colonists took up arms to oppose red-coated troops from Great Britain and mercenaries from Hesse and other principalities. While many city dwellers in other colonies remained loyal to Britain, almost all Virginians were Revolutionists. Of the colonial troops, Virginians accounted for more than 40,000 fighting men from Quebec south to Savannah, and as far west as Illinois. So many were sent north in the early years of the war that alarmed Virginians accused Governor Jefferson of leaving the Old Dominion undefended in his zeal to fulfill General Washington's need for soldiers.

For two years the war engulfed New England and the Middle Atlantic states, where General Henry "Lighthorse Harry" Lee of Westmoreland County, and General Daniel Morgan of Winchester, victor in the battles of Saratoga and Cowpens, won fame.

In another theater of war, General George Rogers Clark of Albemarle and 180 Virginia riflemen in 1779 wrested Virginia's cherished Northwest Territory in the Great Lakes region from the British, who repudiated the claims of Virginia and the other revolting colonies and who now declared

General Henry Lee was nicknamed "Lighthorse Harry" for his cavalry victories. *The Valentine Museum, Richmond.* RIGHT: George Rogers Clark wrested the Northwest Territory from the British in 1779 with only 180 Virginia riflemen.

George Rogers Clark's capture of Vincennes in 1779 defeated British efforts to attach Virginia's Northwest Territory claim to Canada. *Indiana Historical Bureau*

General Daniel Morgan led American troops in the Revolution of Saratoga and Cowpens. *Virginia State Library*

A Virginia rifleman of the Seventh Regiment in frontier uniform during the American Revolution. *Drawing by Peter Copeland. Smithsonian Institution*

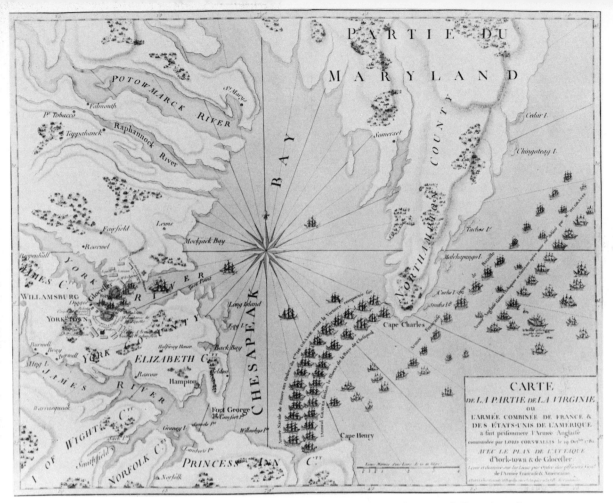

Blockade at the entrance to Chesapeake Bay by the Naval Forces of France under Comte de Grasse, which prevented British forces under Admiral Graves from landing reinforcements for Cornwallis at Yorktown. *Colonial Williamsburg*

it to be a new province of Canada. Clark's victory retained the area for Virginia, under the London Company's 1609 charter, and made it possible for the United States to extend westward without delay after winning the Revolution.

In 1780 the war moved to Virginia. Troops under General Benedict Arnold burned part of Richmond. When the new capital city was threatened a second time, the Assembly adjourned and moved to Charlottesville. A heroic horseback ride by Jack Jouett from Louisa County to Albemarle County in May, 1781, warned Governor Jefferson at Monticello and the General Assembly in Charlottesville in time to avert capture by British cavalry. Jefferson's critics demanded his impeachment for sending so many Virginia troops to fight in the North that Virginia's government was imperiled, but the Governor, with General Washington's support, justified his actions.

The British now prepared to deliver their most massive blow. The commander of its Southern forces, Lieutenant General Earl Cornwallis, prepared to move his troops to Virginia and to join Britain's powerful naval forces at Yorktown. Ex-

As Washington and Rochambeau marched their forces from Williamsburg Cornwallis dug in to resist the siege. He made the home of General Thomas Nelson his headquarters. *Virginia State Library*

plained his Lordship, "I was most firmly persuaded that, until Virginia was reduced, we could not hold the Southern provinces, and that after its reduction, they would fall without more difficulty."

George Washington was familiar with Yorktown's geography, for the port was only fifteen miles from Williamsburg, where he had attended sessions of the Virginia General Assembly. Eagerly he leaped at the chance for a decisive battle with British forces along the York. Conferring with Comte de Rochambeau, who commanded the 7,000 troops France had committed to aid the Americans, he plotted an encirclement which would be supported by French naval forces under Admiral Comte de Grasse. To construct the noose, a French fleet sailed from the West Indies to seal Yorktown off from Chesapeake Bay and prevent reinforcement of Cornwallis' troops by the British fleet. Then Washington marched his worn Continentals from New York to join the colonies' southern army.

To the surprise of the British, DeGrasse's fleet arrived in Chesapeake Bay on September 1 and landed French soldiers. When the British fleet under Admiral Graves attempted to debark British troops, the French dispersed them in a battle off the Virginia Capes, thus cutting off Cornwallis' reinforcements.

Washington and Rochambeau now marched their forces from Williamsburg to Yorktown and encircled Cornwallis' army. The British commander realized his desperate state and dug in to do battle. Five days after Washington's American battery had fired the first shot, the British line began to crack. On October 19 Cornwallis' army surrendered.

To the tune of *The World Turned Upside Down*, it marched out of Yorktown between lines of American and French troops. Onto the quiet field rode British General Charles O'Hara, to offer the sword of the vanquished for Cornwallis, who had pled illness and remained in his camp. Wash-

General Thomas Nelson's house at Yorktown, Cornwallis' headquarters, after the siege. *Virginia State Library*

Artist James Peale's painting of the high officers who won the siege of Yorktown — Lafayette, Washington, Knox, Rochambeau, Hamilton and Tench Tilghman. *Colonial Williamsburg*

ington received it through General Benjamin Lincoln and returned it as a token of respect. The British soldiers then broke ranks to stack their muskets. Men gazed in silent awe, knowing it to be the crowning moment of their lives. British power in American had been broken. American independence was in sight. The taverns of Yorktown and Williamsburg were crowded that night with celebrating people.

As news spread to the colonies, Americans lit bonfires and cheered the victory. King Louis XVI ordered fireworks throughout France. Great Britain's Parliament, badly shaken, declared as "enemies of His Majesty and the country all those who should advise, or by any means attempt, the further prosecution of offensive war on the continent of North America. . . ." Mistaken

policy had lost Britain her American colonies, but it was to force His Majesty's Government to devise a fairer concept of the relationship between motherland and provinces. The eventual British Commonwealth of Nations was essentially that which had been proposed by Richard Bland in his *An Enquiry Into the Rights of the British Colonies* in 1766.

For America, the faith of the people had been rewarded, with the help of France and friends like Lafayette, the German General von Steuben, and the Polish General Kosciusko.

Great Britain signed a provisional treaty of peace with the colonies in Paris a year after the surrender. In it she recognized the existence of a new nation, closely akin to the mother country by heredity but changed by its New World environment. The vision of Raleigh and the men and women who had died to plant a new country was justified, even though Britain no longer would enjoy its benefits.

Peace turned the attention of the liberated colonies to the unclaimed land of the west. Virginia's capital already had moved westward from Williamsburg to Richmond in 1780 to place Governor Jefferson and the Virginia Assembly beyond range of British naval guns. Now the rough trading town laid out by William Byrd I in 1733 was beginning to expand, as Williamsburg had grown ninety years before to absorb the government from Jamestown.

The chief glory of Richmond was its ridges high above the falls of the James River, which recalled the seven hills of Rome. On one of these stood St. John's Church, where Henry had made his "Liberty or Death" speech to the Virginia Convention of 1775. Around it clustered a few houses, built on lots drawn in lotteries conducted by William Byrd III in 1767 and 1768 to pay his gambling debts. On steep streets descending to Shockoe Creek and the James River were other Church Hill homes of tobacco merchants, lawyers, and warehousemen. In the river bottom, along wagon trails which converged at Cary Street and crossed the James on Colonel John Mayo's bridge, stood tobacco warehouses and produce markets.

To Richmond at the end of the Revolution and for many years afterward came farmers from the fertile black belt south of the James, rolling or carting hogsheads of tobacco to be shipped abroad or to be made into pipe tobacco, snuff, cigars, and later into cigarettes. Other drays bearing cattle, wheat, skins, and lumber rolled in from the

William Byrd II inherited Westover and Belvivire from his trader father, the latter becoming the site of the town of Richmond. *Colonial Williamsburg*

eastern counties over County Road (later Main Street) or from the piedmont counties to the west over Broad Road, which later became Broad Street. Flatboats brought other produce down the James to the city, docking and unloading at Westham, above the fall line.

At the northern approach to Mayo's Bridge, at the busy intersection of Pearl (later Fourteenth) and Cary Streets, the infant Commonwealth chose as its temporary Capitol a three-story wooden warehouse. There Virginia attacked the problem of governing its vast domain until a more suitable Capitol could be built on the brow of Richmond Hill. Of Pearl Street, Jefferson wrote in 1789, "There is one street in Richmond (from the bridge straight toward Currie's) which would be considered as

St. John's Church at the top of Church Hill was Richmond's principal building when the Virginia capital was moved to that town in 1780. *The Valentine Museum, Richmond*

handsomely built as any city of Europe."

In their warehouse quarters the Governor and General Assembly made some of the most important decisions in Virginia's history. There the Assembly in 1785 began proceedings which established Kentucky as a state in 1792. There it enacted Jefferson's *Statute for Religious Freedom*, breaking the link between church and state and giving every man the right to believe and worship as he pleased. Tax support was withdrawn from the Anglican Church, and the maintenance of religion was left to individual will, in the tolerant spirit of the Enlightenment which animated many Virginia leaders of the time.

The most important decision of the new Commonwealth, however, was its relinquishment of the Northwest Territory, stretching from the present northern boundary of West Virginia northwestward to the Great Lakes. This claim, which Virginia had cherished since the London Company's charter had been amended in 1609, had often been disputed by other colonies and threatened by foreign powers. Nevertheless, the Old Dominion had maintained her hold for 175 years. Virginia militia under Washington and British regulars under Braddock had fought the French for it. George Rogers Clark had prevented its annexation by Canada in the American Revolution. Now Maryland refused to sign the *Articles of Confederation* unless Virginia relinquished her claim to the territory.

Though Virginia felt the claim to be valid, she now determined to give it up for the sake of the union. At the urging of Jefferson, who dreamed of a chain of states stretching across the continent, the Virginia General Assembly reached its decision:

"We . . . do by these presents convey, transfer, assign, and make over unto the United States in Congress assembled, for the benefit of said States, Virginia inclusive, all right, title, and claim as well of soil as of jurisdiction which the said Commonwealth hath to the territory of tract of country within the limits of the Virginia charter, situate, lying, and being to the Northwest of the River Ohio. . . ."

With this act the era of Virginia's greatest influence in English America began to approach its end.

The aspiration of the new era of independence was symbolized in the building of a new Virginia Capitol to replace the temporary warehouse quarters occupied in Richmond since 1780. In keeping with the soaring spirit of the new American age, it took the form of a Roman temple. From France, where he had served since his gubernatorial term as American minister, Jefferson persuaded the legislators to build an

Transporting tobacco to Richmond, the principal warehouse center and shipping port for the crop. Growers brought their product by barge, wagon and rolling hogshead.
Virginia State Library

The completed Capitol gave Richmond the first example of the classical revival in architecture in the United States. The style was used in building the formal structures of the city of Washington. *The Valentine Museum, Richmond*

A warehouse adjoining the bridge at Pearl and Cary Streets became the temporary capitol of Virginia after removal from Williamsburg. Governors Thomas Jefferson, Thomas Nelson, Jr., Benjamin Harrison, Patrick Henry and Edmund Randolph served here. *The Valentine Museum, Richmond*

Jefferson sent from France a plaster model for the new Capitol of Virginia. It was erected with modifications in 1789. *Virginia State Library*

adaptation of the ancient Maison Carré, at Nimes. With his usual vision and sense of history, he sent a plaster model of the suggested Capitol from France to Virginia to show legislators how it should be built.

When the Capitol was completed in 1789 it gave Virginia the first example of classical revival architecture in America, and it set the style for the federal city of Washington when it was reared soon afterward. Virginia in these years set a standard for the nation.

Tobacco growers originated the rolling hogshead for taking tobacco to the shipping ports. Moving over the "Tobacco Road," one hogshead could hold 400 to 500 pounds of tobacco leaf, often a small farmer's whole crop. Such rolling vehicles had to halt a mile from deep water for inspection of the condition of the contents, which often suffered from travel over muddy roads.

8   States and Statesmen in Transition

VIRGINIA STATESMEN IN THE NEW REPUBLIC: *A great generation of Virginians, born in colonialism and educated by English standards, leads in developing a constitution and a structure for the new republic. George Washington is president of the convention. Madison contributes greatly to the Constitution, and Jefferson suggests the Bill of Rights. John Marshall as Chief Justice establishes a strong basis of government by law, assuring traditional Anglo-Saxon rights. Four of the first five Presidents and five of the first seven Secretaries of State are Virginians. Concepts of self-government, human dignity, and individual rights and responsibilities which the first colonists brought from England are built into the new order. As a border state between the commercial North and agricultural South, Virginia has power even beyond that assured by its dominant size and population.*

States and Statesmen in Transition

During the struggle with Great Britain, some Americans continued to hope for an accommodation that would leave them in the British empire. Many Northern colonists remained loyal to England and moved to Canada, which was still British. However, majority sentiment of Virginia hardened early into a desire for independence. Washington, Jefferson, Madison, Mason, Edmund Randolph, and Richard Henry Lee were thinking throughout the Revolution of the type of government that would best serve the colonies after victory was won. Waging a war with inadequate money and troops under the colonies' loose *Articles of Confederation* had convinced them that greater

solidarity was necessary. After all, Spain still sought colonies in the New World.

Accustomed to think in terms of continental development, most Virginia leaders favored an expandable federation of states. However, they differed widely in their views on the powers which should be given by the states to the central government.

Writing from Mount Vernon to provincial governors, Washington urged a strong central power. "We are either a united people under one head and for federal purposes, or we are thirteen independent sovereignties, eternally counteracting each other," he observed.

Disagreement between Maryland and

Virginia's Northwest Territory, as curtailed by the claims of Connecticut to a slice running west to the Mississippi River, is depicted in this map that Abel Buell dedicated to the "Governor and Company" of Connecticut in 1785. *New Jersey Historical Society*

Virginia in 1785 over use of the Potomac River gave Washington opportunity to invite representatives of the two states to Mount Vernon, and this led Virginia to call a conference of provinces. The outgrowth was a convention in Annapolis and eventually another in Philadelphia for the announced purpose of amending the Articles of Confederation. However, with unspoken consent from most provinces, the convention which met in Independence Hall in Philadelphia in 1787 did a great deal more.

Virginia was first to accept the invitation and sent the ablest of her Revolutionary leaders except for Jefferson, who was still in France, and Patrick Henry, who "smelt a rat." Washington headed Virginia's delegation and was named the convention's president. Most constructive of the delegates was James Madison, then 36, whose native brilliance had been sharpened by service in the Virginia Assembly and in the Continental Congress. The eloquent Edmund Randolph was chosen by Virginia representatives to present their proposals.

These called for creation of a union of limited central powers. To protect states against the tyranny of any region or interest, the powers of the executive, legislative, and judicial branches were carefully specified and compartmented. A Congress of two houses was proposed, one based on proportional representation to protect the big states and the other with uniform state representation to protect the small.

The plan was chiefly Madison's creation, to which George Mason, George Wythe, and Randolph also contributed. The sixth Virginia delegate was John Blair of Wil-

James Madison was the principal author of the plan for union that Virginia submitted to the Constitutional Convention. *Colonial Williamsburg*

liamsburg, great-nephew of Commissary Blair of William and Mary and son of a John Blair who had been president of the Virginia Council of State and acting Governor.

Dr. James McClurg of Richmond and John Blair II of Williamsburg were among the delegates Virginia sent to the Constitutional Convention. Others were George Washington, George Mason, George Wythe, Edmund Randolph and James Madison. *Virginia Historical Society*

(The younger Blair was to become Associate Justice of the United States Supreme Court by appointment of President Washington in 1790, serving until 1796.) The seventh was Dr. James McClurg, a Richmond physician of Federalist sentiment, who was chosen after Henry declined.

The Virginia plan was debated at length, for the smaller provinces' fear of domination by Virginia and Massachusetts almost wrecked hope of union. However, Madison showed that the significant difference lay not in the size of the states but in their economies. The large provinces insisted that appropriation and salary measures originate in the House of Representatives to prevent small states from imposing unnecessary taxes through the Senate. As a compromise, the convention concluded that "All bills for raising revenue shall originate in the House of Representatives; but the Senate may propose or concur as on other bills."

Pressing for necessary agreement, Virginia under Madison's leadership urged that states be admitted to the union from the Northwest Territory under the same unconditional terms as the first thirteen. Stout old Gouverneur Morris of Pennsylvania disagreed; he was able to limit the commitment to the mere statement that "New States may be admitted by the Congress into this Union." The critical question as to whether Congress could limit the powers of future states was thus left unresolved, paving the way for abolitionist efforts to prohibit slavery in Missouri when that territory sought admittance to the union in 1820.

Because of the Virginians' effort to avoid dissension, the issue of slavery was not discussed except to determine the basis for direct taxation and for representation in Congress. Between the demands of Georgia and South Carolina that all slaves be counted and Northern insistence that none should be, the convention compromised on three-fifths. At the urging of Georgia and the Carolinas, control over importation of slaves into the United States was left to individual

Young James Monroe and aging Benjamin Harrison voted against ratification of the Constitution by Virginia. Harrison signed the Declaration of Independence and was the father of William Henry Harrison, and great grandfather of Benjamin Harrison, both later Presidents. *Colonial Williamsburg*

GEORGE WASHINGTON. GENL HENRY KNOX, Secy. of War. ALEXANDER HAMILTON, Secy. of the Treasury. THOMAS JEFFERSON, Secy. of State. EDMUND RANDOLPH, Attorney General.

WASHINGTON AND HIS CABINET.

Washington and his Cabinet, as portrayed by Currier & Ives. The members were General Henry Knox of Massachusetts, Secretary of War; Alexander Hamilton of New York, Secretary of the Treasury; Thomas Jefferson of Virginia, Secretary of State and Edmund Randolph of Virginia, Attorney General. *New York Historical Society*

states until 1808, although Congress was empowered to impose an import duty of $10 a head at any time.

Sectionalism first intruded ominously in the debate over the power which Congress should be given to regulate commerce. On this issue, which turned George Mason against the Constitution and later almost persuaded Virginia's ratifying convention to reject the document, the Virginians feared enactment of tariffs which would protect Northern industry and discourage continued European purchase of the South's cotton and tobacco.

They recalled the British Navigation Acts' injury to agriculture by raising export-import costs through limitation of shipping to British vessels. Southern delegates therefore voted not to permit enactment of tariffs and navigation laws by mere majority vote; they demanded approval by at least two-thirds of both houses. The only

States and Statesmen in Transition [145]

assurance they could obtain, however, was a prohibition against the levy by Congress of duties on exports. Over objection of Southern representatives, the other provinces were strong enough to empower Congress to compel shipment of American goods in American ships by simple majority vote, if so desired.

Though the Constitution's framers often divided by regions, they reacted as individuals to the underlying issue of the convention: What powers of the new nation should be exercised by central government and what powers should be retained by the states? Military men like Washington and Alexander Hamilton favored strong central government, while those of agrarian background like George Mason maintained the Whigs' belief in local powers. Between ultra-nationalists on one extreme and localists on the other, most delegates were in-between. They were open to persuasion by the convention's leaders: James Wilson and Gouverneur Morris of Pennsylvania, William Paterson of New Jersey, Rufus King and Roger Sherman of Massachusetts, Charles Cotesworth Pinckney of South Carolina, and Madison, Mason, and Edmund Randolph of Virginia.

The result of weeks of debate was a document whose broad principles created a revolutionary new nation but left unresolved many details of Federal-State relationship in the effort to obtain ratification by state conventions. In this irresolution was the seed of civil war.

Delegates to the Constitutional Convention debated issues which had faced Virginians since 1607: What powers should be exercised locally and which by the central government? Which should be the responsibility of executive and which of the legis-

lature? Should the judiciary have power to overrule acts of government? Should government have power to control the livelihood of farmers, manufacturers, and shippers through taxation and regulation? Finally, and of importance to most Virginians because of their espousal of the philosophy of Locke and the French rationalists: How could a new nation's need for order be reconciled with a man's need for freedom?

True to Virginia's libertarian political sentiment, most of her representatives in Philadelphia favored the greatest individual freedom under law. Jefferson and Madison were to make these principles the basis for those who came to be known in the eighteenth century by Republicans and in the nineteenth as Democrats.

Most of Virginia's Revolutionary leaders had supported the move for a Federal government. However, the issues discussed in Independence Hall and reported in the press now alarmed many of her people, who felt that some of the sovereign rights that had been jealously guarded by the old colony were being abridged by compromises proposed by other states. The prolonged debate in Virginia's ratifying convention which met in Richmond in 1788 was not won until nine other provinces had approved ratification, providing the necessary minimum for creation of the United States. Even then Virginia approved only by vote of 89 to 79.

In no other state convention was the proposed union subjected to such attack as in that which met on Richmond's Capitol Hill. Leading the opposition was George Mason, who argued that Virginia and the South could not afford to give Congress the crucial power to control national commerce by simple majority vote and thus protect Northern industry with tariffs. Other opponents included James Monroe, Benjamin Harrison, and Judge John Tyler, the latter two fathers of Presidents-to-be. The most persuasive voice of all was Patrick Henry's.

No man in America could equal the eloquence of the fiery Hanover attorney. Article by article, he showed how Virginia would lose power to the nation. And article by article, James Madison counteracted his arguments. So compelling was Madison's logic that he gradually convinced the majority of delegates that the weaknesses of the Constitution were not fatal. A young Richmond attorney, John Marshall, also proved a strong debater, while General Lighthorse Harry Lee and Edmund Randolph, now Governor and a convert to the cause of ratification, gave support. Washington had refused to be a delegate, but Federalists circulated a letter in which he had written, "I am fully persuaded . . . that it [the Constitution] or disunion is before us."

Only after Madison had promised to attempt amendment of the Constitution as originally drafted by obtaining Congressional adoption of a bill of "inalienable rights" to protect individual liberties and property rights did the Virginia Convention give reluctant approval. Even then it added this proviso:

"We, the delegates of the people of Virginia . . . do, in the name and in behalf of the People of Virginia, declare and make known, that the powers granted under the Constitution, being derived from the people of the United States, may be resumed by them whensoever the same shall be perverted to their injury or oppression, and that every power not granted thereby remains with them and at their will;

that therefore no right of any denomination can be cancelled, abridged, restrained, or modified by the Congress . . . or any department of or officer of the United States, except in those instances in which power is given by the Constitution for those purposes; and that, among other essential rights, the liberty of conscience and of the press cannot be cancelled, abridged, restrained, or modified by any authority of the United States."

At the American ministry in France, Thomas Jefferson kept his usual vigil over Virginia's affairs. On Madison's assurance, he sent to his Virginia supporters his qualified support for ratification, provided that guarantees of basic individual rights could be added to it, as Mason had written for Virginia's constitution of 1776.

Although the plucky little Madison was defeated by antifederalist vote in the Virginia General Assembly for one of Virginia's two seats in the first United States Senate, he won popular election to the House of Representatives and there obtained adoption in 1791 of the first ten amendments to the Constitution, embodying Virginia's proposed Bill of Rights.

The sectionalism which arose in the Constitutional debates increased as the machinery of union began to function. As a colony, Virginia had felt herself to be first. Now she was reduced to a common political level. Her people's pride in their pioneering and their primacy made many of them resentful of union. In the words of Patrick Henry, "They were Virginians first." A more realistic concern was for the future of slavery, the basis of Virginia's agriculture — indeed, of her whole economy. Increasingly, the Old Dominion and the other states which depended on slave labor were conscious that they were outnumbered. A new awareness of human rights, generated by the Revolu-

By compromise between Jefferson and Hamilton, the new national capital was located on the Potomac River between Virginia and Maryland. The seat of government moved there in 1800. *Virginia State Library*

tion, made Americans more sensitive to the incongruity of slavery in a nation dedicated to political equality.

Virginia had entered the Constitutional debates with confidence; she emerged shaken by prophecies of her decline which came from Patrick Henry, George Mason, and Richard Henry Lee. After a struggle, she had been persuaded by Madison and Marshall to ratify the Constitution, but she could see the beginning of an eclipse of state powers. Virginians knew union was necessary, but the reservations of her conservatives stirred an uneasy fear that the Constitution had created too strong a central power. The growing difference between commercial North and agricultural South pointed to trouble.

To protect the states and preserve the union, Jefferson and Madison argued in their lifetime that the state governments were "co-equals" of the national government in every area except foreign affairs. During his service as Secretary of State in Washington's cabinet beginning in 1789, Jefferson first pressed this doctrine, but with little effect. When John Adams succeeded Washington in the presidency in 1797, the Jeffersonians saw opportunity to limit the growth of nationalism by creating an alliance between Southern agriculturists and Northern workingmen. Their strategy was to outvote the Federalist propertied interests, chiefly in the Northern states, which supported the economic policies of Secretary of the Treasury Alexander Hamilton.

Development during John Adams' term of this coalition was the beginning of political parties in the United States. It was also the beginning of a sectional division which nearly destroyed the union. The hapless Adams provided the Jeffersonians with the issue which they needed by his administration's sponsorship of the Alien and

Sedition Acts of 1798, which violated Constitutional limits by subjecting newspaper critics of government to unreasonable libel provisions and limiting freedom to the press. Through the Kentucky legislator John Breckenridge, Jefferson encouraged the General Assembly of that state in 1798 to pass resolutions declaring part of the laws "altogether void and of no effect" and asserting the "right" of a state to reject such a law. Jefferson sent a copy of the resolves to Madison, who drew up similar resolutions. These were passed the same year by the Virginia Assembly calling on other states to co-operate with Virginia "in maintaining unimpaired the authority, rights, and liberties reserved to the states. . . ."

John Marshall, campaigning in Richmond for Congress as a supporter of Adams, declared that he "never saw such intemperance as existed in the Virginia Assembly."

A political swap between Jefferson and Hamilton in this period placed the capital of the new republic in the District of Columbia, on land provided for that purpose by Virginia and Maryland. Through the cession of her Northwest Territory in 1784, Virginia had received funds which paid off most of her Revolutionary debt. Hamilton now convinced his fellow cabinet member, Jefferson, that unless the federal treasury assumed the debts of the other states, they would secede. In return for Jefferson and Madison's reluctant support of assumption of the states' debts, Hamilton used his influence to establish the national capital along the Potomac River, on the Maryland-Virginia boundary. The seat of government

Thomas Jefferson as President was a moderate nationalist who tried to reconcile the interest of the states with that of the nation. *Colonial Williamsburg* RIGHT: John Marshall favored a strong central government and as Chief Justice of the United States added to the national power over Jefferson's opposition. *The Valentine Museum, Richmond*

was moved from Philadelphia in 1800, and John Adams' wife Abigail hung the family wash in the East Room of the new White House.

In the first thirty-six years of union, a Virginian filled the Presidency for all except John Adams' four years. The concept of party government which Jefferson originated had not fully crystallized, and Washington, Jefferson, Madison, and Monroe in turn moved cautiously to maintain the balance of interests which held the states together. Even the once-partisan Jefferson minimized as President the differences he had once exploited earlier in defeating John Adams. "We are all Republicans, we are all Federalists," he blandly told the crowd at his first inauguration in 1801.

Despite the preponderance of Virginians in high office — five of the first seven Secretaries of State, for example — the years of the so-called Virginia Dynasty culminated in an Era of Good Feeling in which the new nation admitted eight new states, expanded its territory, and rapidly developed the West.

But the triumph of the Jeffersonians' strict construction of the Constitution was short-lived. While the Jeffersonians were advocating "co-equal" state and federal powers, the Supreme Court of the United States was steadily strengthening the national government from the inside. Its guiding genius was former Congressman John Marshall of Richmond, who had helped Madison achieve Virginia's ratification of the Constitution in 1787.

George Washington directs his field hands at Mount Vernon. The early Virginia-born Presidents were plantation owners and favored the physical expansion of the nation. *Thomas L. Williams*

Plantation houses multiplied in nineteenth-century Virginia, but most of them were smaller than those of the earlier "tobacco millionaires." *Thomas L. Williams*

Appointed to the court by President John Adams in recognition of his Federalism, Marshall was now able to offset the strict constructionist views on the constitution of his distant cousin, Jefferson, with whom he had disagreed all his life on nearly every subject. On one major issue after another, the Supreme Court under his lead reversed or thwarted Jefferson and the pro-Jeffersonian Congress. In his effect on American life, Marshall as Chief Justice proved as influential as Jefferson as President.

It was ironic that in Virginia's capital at Richmond, where Jefferson had served as Governor during the Revolution, Marshall had become the voice of nationalism since Washington's death in 1799 at Mount Vernon. Because Marshall was Richmond's leading public figure, Jefferson avoided Richmond and depended on his lieutenants, Chief Justice Spencer Roane of the Virginia Supreme Court of Appeals and editor Thomas Ritchie of the *Richmond Enquirer*, to combat Marshall's influence as best they could.

During the trial of Aaron Burr for treason in the United States Circuit Court in Richmond in 1807 (sitting, to be sure, in the newly completed Virginia Capitol), bitterness between the cousins reached its height when Chief Justice Marshall issued a subpoena for the President's appearance in court. Jefferson ignored it.

Despite the appearance of sectionalism, Virginia was still the most influential power in the union when John Quincy Adams succeeded Monroe as President in 1825. Like imperial Rome, her statesmen and generals led the nation in its rapid expansion. Almost single-handed, New England was beginning to create an American literature; her greatest writers — Emerson, Hawthorne, Longfellow, Whittier, Thoreau, and Lowell — were all born between 1803 and 1819. New York and Philadelphia were cornering the nation's commerce. In the realm of public service, however, Virginia in these years was unexcelled. "Oh! those Virginians are noble spirits," the Boston patriot Oxenbridge Thacher said of them.

The best and worst of Virginia at this period was observed by William Ellery Channing in 1798, after he had come from Harvard College to Chesterfield County to teach in the household of David Meade Randolph, at Ampthill. "Here I find great vices but greater virtues," wrote the future Unitarian leader. "There is one single trait that attaches me . . . more than all the virtues of New England. They *love money less* than we do. . . . They are more disinterested. . . . Could I only take from Virginians their sensuality and their slaves, I should think them the greatest people in the world."

In the census of 1800, Virginia led the sixteen states of the nation in population,

Richmond in the early nineteenth century, romantically embellished by the painter
Cooke, was dominated by the new State Capitol, where many battles for states' rights
were fought. *The Valentine Museum, Richmond*

wealth, and size, just as she had since the beginning of English America. By 1820, however, she lost her place as the most populous state. In that year New York had increased through European immigration to 1,372,812 residents, while Virginia numbered 1,065,336, including slaves. Close behind Virginia was Pennsylvania with 1,049,458 residents.

In the growth of population and industry of the North could be seen the approaching eclipse of Virginia.

Two leading Jeffersonians in early nineteenth century Virginia were Thomas Ritchie, left, editor of the Richmond Enquirer, and his cousin, Chief Justice Spencer Roane of the Virginia Supreme Court. *The Valentine Museum, Richmond*

A sketch of shipping at Norfolk in the late eighteenth century. Norfolk was a leading competitor of Richmond for Virginia's commerce. *City of Norfolk*

9 'The Sceptre of Virginia' Passes

Virginia Builds Toward Nationhood: *The ambitious conception of Sir Walter Raleigh is realized as Americans spread across the continent and acquire Spanish Florida and French Louisiana by purchase. From the original colony of Virginia are formed the states of Kentucky in 1792, Ohio in 1803, Indiana in 1816, Illinois in 1818, and part of North Dakota in 1859. In 1863 the western part of the state becomes West Virginia. Reduced in size and people, Virginia loses much of its political and economic influence as the center of American population moves westward.*

9

'The Sceptre of Virginia' Passes

The United States moved in the nineteenth century into the company of the great nations. President Jefferson in 1803 bought the Louisiana Territory from France and doubled the United States' size for $15,000,000. President Monroe in 1819 purchased Florida from Spain and also acquired Spanish claims to the Oregon Country. These new lands stimulated the westward movement. Further momentum was added to this expansion in 1823, when New York opened the Erie Canal, providing water transport from the midwest to New York City and opening up the Great Lakes region.

A healthy textile industry and shipping trade developed in New England in the new century to replace trade with Great Britain. Like the South's agriculture, these Northern interests were badly hurt by the embargo against trade with Great Britain that President Jefferson imposed in 1807 in an effort to halt British seizure of American seamen and to avert another war with Britain, which nevertheless broke out in 1812. However, the Northern states turned the embargo to their advantage by developing a domestic economy, while the agricultural South merely sat and suffered.

A wave of equalitarian democracy, stirred up by resentment of Great Britain, made British ways of life anathema to the majority of Americans, who accepted Jef-

Henry Clay, leading Kentucky statesman and Secretary of State under John Quincy Adams, was reared at The Slashes in Hanover County, Virginia. *Thomas L. Williams*

ferson's design for the new America. Any but the simplest mode of dress and social behavior was considered to be "aristocratic" and therefore un-American. As a consequence of the new democratic spirit, slavery seemed out of place. New England intellectuals began to ask a question that became the century's insistent issue: How could a slave enjoy "life, liberty, and the pursuit of happiness," promised to Americans by the *Declaration of Independence?*

The change in social climate weakened the position of the South. Abundant new land and the deluge of European immigrants in the North clearly threatened the South's agriculture. It was clear that New England and the middle Atlantic states benefitted from their diversified economy, while the

South stood still. Virginians could not overcome their inherited preference for rural life. All over America except in the South and on the frontier, the businessman was replacing the planter as the agent of America's growth. Yet Virginia stuck to farming despite the decline in land productivity which only a few scientific planters, like John Taylor of Caroline and Edmund Ruffin of Hanover, were beginning to combat through knowledge of soil chemistry.

The English tone of eastern Virginia discouraged the growth of commerce there and drove many ambitious young men to other areas. The rolls of William and Mary, Hampden-Sydney, and Washington College were filled with names of Virginia-born students who migrated in the Revolutionary period to new land in the west and south. The partial observance in colonial Virginia of the English practice of primogeniture, which favored the eldest son in dispersing a family's estate, encouraged younger sons to migrate to frontier lands, just as it had encouraged younger scions of English families to venture to Virginia.

In a 150-year period beginning in 1774, at least 329 men born within Virginia's present boundaries served other states as delegates to the Continental Congress, as United States Senators, and as Representatives in Congress. The greatest number — fifty-eight — represented Kentucky. Among these were such men as Henry Clay, John Marshall's brother Humphrey Marshall, and John Breckinridge, sponsor of the Kentucky Resolutions of 1798 and grandfather of Vice President John Cabell Breckinridge, who served from 1857 until 1861. In the same period, twenty-six prominent Georgia lawmakers were born in the Old Dominion, including William Harris Crawford, whose

Many Virginians emigrated to Texas. Stephen Austin, left, became a founder of the settlement and Sam Houston was first president of the Texas republic in 1836. *Virginia State Library*

family moved south from the Blue Ridge Mountains early in the century and who was Vice President under Monroe. In Tennessee, John Sevier and thirty others were Virginia-born. Missouri, North Carolina, Louisiana, Mississippi, Alabama, South Carolina, Maryland, and Texas also enjoyed a steady influx from Virginia.

From Wythe County, Virginia, Stephen Fuller Austin moved with his father Moses Austin to become a founder of Texas in 1822. From his birthplace near Lexington, in Rockbridge County, Sam Houston migrated in 1806 to Tennessee and later to Texas, where he became a United States general and first president of the Republic of Texas in 1836.

John Breckinridge, left, was born near Staunton, Virginia, and moved west. He introduced the Kentucky Resolutions in the legislature of that state in 1798 and became Attorney General under Jefferson. William Harris Crawford moved from Virginia to Georgia and became Vice President under Monroe and a candidate for President later. *Virginia State Library*

James Madison retired from the Presidency to his plantation, Montpelier, near Charlottesville, not far from Jefferson. *Virginia Chamber of Commerce*

Throughout the new states, homesick emigrants tried to preserve at least a little of their past by naming their new homes for scenes they had left behind. Many a midwestern state acquired a Mount Vernon, a Monticello, or a Montpelier. Eighteen hamlets across the land were given the name Jamestown, and twelve were called Williamsburg. In the same way the settlers of 1607 had transplanted English place-names to the shores of the James River and Chesapeake Bay.

Of all the new states, Kentucky bore Virginia's image most strongly. A long history of exploration and pioneering preceded Virginia's cession of the territory and its statehood in 1792. As early as 1756, Andrew Lewis of Augusta County, a native of Ireland who had settled in the Valley of Virginia, led a detachment of Virginians and Cherokee scouts into the region to rout the savage Shawnees from the Ohio River area. After eighteen more years of intermittent warfare with Indians in the area, Lewis led two regiments of Virginia militia in 1774, on orders of Governor Dunmore, and defeated the Indians decisively at Point Pleasant, at the mouth of the Kanawha River in the present West Virginia.

This victory drove the Indians west of the Ohio River and encouraged settlers to cross the mountains. Harrodsburg was founded in 1774, Boonesborough in 1775, and Fort Nelson in 1781, on the present site of Louisville. The huge Virginia county of Kentucky was created in 1776.

Once the Indians had been driven off, land companies and families rushed to settle there. One of the first settlements was made through the effort of the young Indian fighter Daniel Boone. The wiry woodsman almost single-handedly extended the settlers' path from the Holston River, at the present southwest tip of Virginia, to the Kentucky River near Louisville. Variously called the Wilderness Road, the Virginia Traders' Path, the Kentucky Road, and finally the Valley Pike, this historic route for two centuries enabled pioneers to move through Virginia from Wadkin's Ferry southwestward through the Valley of Virginia. Threading the narrow Cumberland Gap, they passed into the present Kentucky. First Indians, then traders like Abraham Wood and William Byrd I, and finally settlers followed its course. It was the umbilicus

Migrants from Virginia to Kentucky built their first fort at Boonesborough, named for Daniel Boone, in 1775. *Kentucky Department of Information*

through which Kentucky was nurtured.

Southwest Virginia and Kentucky were peopled by cross-currents of English descendants from eastern Virginia and Scotch-Irish Presbyterians. The latter were Scotsmen who had first emigrated from Northern Ireland to Pennsylvania in the mid-seventeenth century. In search of cheap land, successive generations moved southward over the Wilderness Road into the Valley of Virginia and finally into Kentucky.

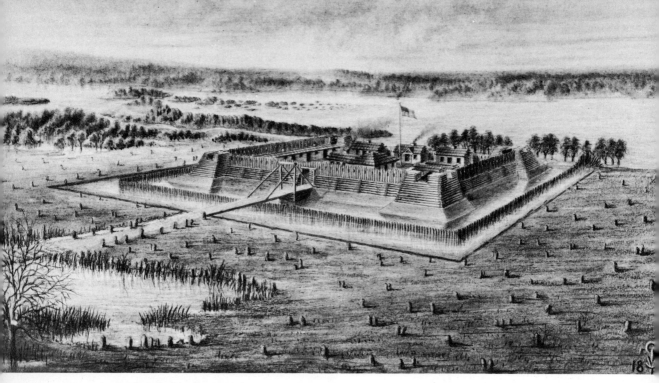

Settlers built a fort on the present site of Louisville in 1782 and named it Fort Nelson for Virginia's Governor Thomas Nelson, Jr. *The Filson Club, Louisville*

These hardy people were used to rigorous schooling, hard work, and piety. They toughened the fibre of Virginia's western outreach. By "simple living and high thinking," they planted churches and schools through the Valley and into the highlands of the Appalachian Mountains. Many of their early log or stone academies grew into universities and gave a Scottish cast to education in the upper South.

Presbyterianism was the faith of the Virginia frontier, just as Anglicanism had been the religion of the first colonists in 1607. The adherents of John Knox led the western movement until Baptists became numerous in the colonies after 1750 and Methodists began their strong growth in the Revolution. The Anglicans, renamed Episcopalians in America after the Revolution, were over-whelmed by anti-British sentiment and the loss of church lands. They felt the loss of Loyalist ministers who returned to England, leaving pulpits vacant. Many former Anglicans now lost interest in the ancient forms and ceremonies of the Church of England and joined other denominations.

When a wave of Protestant fundamentalism rolled through the South after the Revolution, many Episcopal parishioners joined the Baptists and Methodists. Forgotten was the easy conviviality of Anglican Virginia's horse-racing, card-playing, and evenings warmed by port and madeira. The new puritanism demanded Sunday abstinence from all social pleasures. In the revolt against the religious liberalism of earlier generations, some Episcopal congregations re-constituted themselves as Baptists or Methodists.

Except for the German Lutherans of the Valley and a scattering of Quakers throughout the State, these Protestant sects accounted for most Virginians. Roman Catholics were few. The European immigrants who transplanted Catholicism to the Northern states in the nineteenth century were discouraged by competing slave labor from coming to Virginia.

Population in parts of eastern Virginia dwindled after 1800 as planters moved south and west in search of richer farmland. This migration was increased after Eli Whitney invented the cotton gin in 1793, stimulating the demand of British mills for the fibre and luring former tobacco planters to seek new cotton land. Unfortunately for Virginia, the boom in agriculture created by cotton in the 1820s and '30s increased the need for slaves and prevented the crystallization of sentiment to free and repatriate Virginia's Negroes, which Jefferson had proposed to the General Assembly in 1776.

Virginia's population west of the Blue Ridge increased greatly, but the entrenched power of eastern planters continued to control the state. Since adoption of the Virginia Constitution in 1776, each county had had

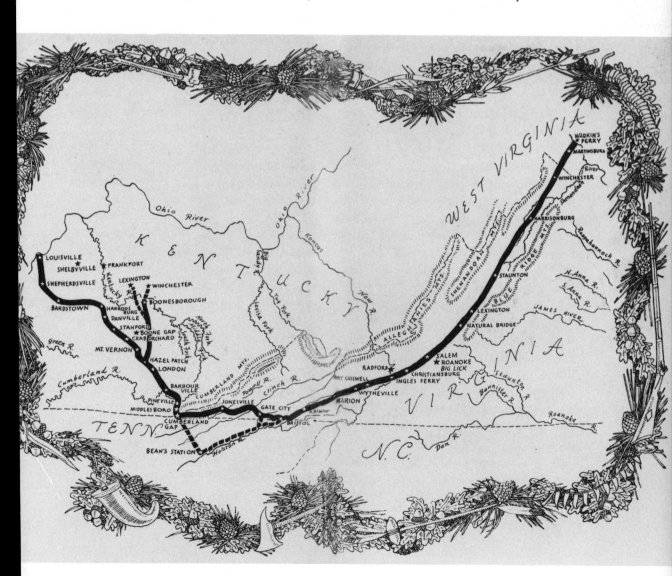

The great thoroughfare from Virginia into the Kentucky territory was the Wilderness Road, along the Valley of Virginia and over the mountains through the Cumberland Gap. From *The Wilderness Road*, by permission of Mrs. Robert L. Kincaid

two representatives in the House of Delegates. Despite the greater population of the huge western counties such as Kentucky, Tidewater legislators were unwilling to share control of the State government. Virginia's failure to keep pace with its western citizens' needs in the nineteenth century was the beginning of an alienation which was to dismember what remained of the state after Kentucky and the Northwestern Territory had been ceded.

Western Virginia made its first organized protest in 1816. Spokesmen for more than thirty mountain counties met at Staunton, in the Valley of Virginia, and petitioned the General Assembly for a new State constitution which would give them representation in Federal and State elections in proportion to their population. They pointed out that all of western Virginia had only four State senators to thirteen for the east, in spite of the fact that more free

Virginians lived west of the Blue Ridge Mountains than east of them.

The westerners finally forced the calling of a State Constitutional Convention at Richmond in 1829. This "last gathering of the giants" numbered among its delegates Chief Justice John Marshall, former Presidents Madison and Monroe, and Representative John Randolph of Roanoke. With Monroe presiding, the westerners were able to wring from eastern delegates more liberal voting laws, a greater representation in the General Assembly, and a curtailment of the powers of the Council of State which had survived since Jamestown as an appointive advisory body to the Governor. These concessions, while beneficial to the west, fell short of westerners' demands.

Control of Virginia was so securely anchored in the eastern part of the state that the westerners felt their interests to be neglected. So completely were eastern States'

Mountainous southwest Virginia was settled by cross-currents of English and Scots descendants. Its small farms supported a farm life quite different from that of the eastern plantations. *Virginia State Library*

Rightists in command that the outlanders increasingly looked to the federal government in Washington for public improvements which they needed. Sentiment began to grow for separating the western counties into a new state. Like the smoldering question of slavery, the issue was such an emotional one that it could not be discussed objectively on either side.

Where were the men to lead Virginia in this difficult age? Washington, Henry, and George Mason were dead. Jefferson and Madison had never recovered support they had lost in Virginia in the failure of the Embargo in 1807, which cut off foreign purchase of Virginia's crops. Monroe, like both, was too old for the new generation. Marshall was restrained from open politics by his judicial office. The able Edmund Randolph, so effective in the Constitutional Convention, had dropped out of national affairs with his resignation from Washing-

ton's cabinet in 1795 on the accusation of mishandling funds. Younger Virginia statesmen seemed pale in the shadow of these survivors of the Great Generation.

What failure of will beset Virginia in the critical years after the Missouri Compromise? The question puzzled observers then and now. Slavery, sectionalism, and political control of the state for too long by too few men all played a part. Beyond this was the fact that resentment had developed toward Virginia's long rule, particularly the passing of the Presidency from Jefferson to Madison to Monroe.

The simplest explanation is exhaustion. Leadership in American affairs since 1765 had cost Virginia dearly. Her concessions to nationhood had gradually embittered Virginia conservatives, who had already become more opposed to the direction of national policy. Dismayed by years of agricultural loss, many influential Virginians

'The Sceptre of Virginia' Passes [167]

The individualist John Randolph was a strong states' rights advocate and critic of both Jefferson and Marshall. This reproduction of a famous silhouette shows him on his stud farm, Roanoke. *Thomas L. Williams*

had become defensive and reactionary. Young men who sensed the spirit of the age were leaving the state and going west. "All the independent young men are leaving," one Virginian wrote.

So long as a Virginian had been in the White House, the Old Dominion had responded to the Jeffersonian party. Fearing the strength of the growing North, Jefferson, Madison, and Monroe in turn had demanded adherence to Constitutional limits on the national government's power. However, after slavery became all-consuming, resistance to party leadership increased in Virginia and the South. Talk of States' Rights increased, and Senator John C. Calhoun of South Carolina became spokesman for a growing nullification spirit. The story of Virginia from 1820 to 1861 is the story of the triumph of Calhoun's sectionalism over the moderate nationalism of Jefferson and Madison.

Calhoun and his extremists won most of the South in the Era of Division that followed Monroe's Era of Good Feeling. In her characteristic effort to find middle ground, Virginia attempted to moderate a growing hostility between North and South. However, the issues of slavery and nullification stirred the deepest emotions of voters, and the achievement of any agreement was difficult.

Opinion within Virginia herself was split. So long as Virginians held public office, her voters remained loyal to the Jeffersonians. However, when Andrew Jackson took over Jefferson's party in 1829 many Virginians resented his high-handed methods and bolted. In violation of principles some began to vote with the unionist National Republicans and their successors, the New Whigs, who became the party of

properted people that the Federalists once had been. Others remained with Jackson's Democrats. From the end of the Virginia dynasty until after the Civil War, the old planter consensus that had governed Virginia since Jamestown was splintered.

During the administration of Jackson and until the outbreak of the Civil War, Virginia was a wasp's nest of political individualists. Cliques, intrastate sectionalism, and personal vendettas destroyed much of the power she once had wielded in national affairs. In describing a typical Virginia Congressman of the period, John Quincy Adams wrote: "His delight was the consciousness of his own independence."

The Virginia spectrum extended from the anarchism of Representative John Randolph of Roanoke on the one hand to the nationalism of John Marshall on the other. In between them ranged the majority of the Virginians, whose views were best represented for much of this period by a group of Jeffersonians known as the Richmond Junto.

On the left, Randolph's extreme strict-constructionists called themselves the Tertium Quids, or "Third Force," and were at home in no party. They were extreme examples of Virginia's traditional opposition to central power. Though a cousin through the Randolphs to both Jefferson and Marshall, the irascible John derided Jefferson as "an authority of nothing except plows," and refused to follow his party leadership in Virginia or in Congress. He was so agitated by the Missouri statehood debate in Congress that for days he could eat only gruel and crackers.

Randolph urged the South to secede rather than accept limitation on slavery. "Asking one of the states to surrender part of her sovereignty," he rasped, "is like asking a lady to surrender part of her chastity." In the same vein as had Patrick Henry, George Mason, and Richard Henry Lee, Randolph resisted nationalism. "I am an aristrocrat," he boasted. "I love liberty. I hate equality!" He boasted that Virginia came first in his affections, then England, and then the rest of the "old thirteen States."

Other Quids were Senators William Branch Giles, of Petersburg, a sometime follower of Jefferson, and John Taylor of Caroline. Taylor typified many Southern legislators in his insistence on a simplicity and economy in government which not even the frugal administrations of Jefferson, Madison, and Monroe were able to achieve. Nevertheless, his long and turgid essays, signed "Arator," were a contribution toward the scientific agriculture which Virginia needed to regain place in the sun.

The moderate nationalists in Virginia politics were typified by the Richmond Junto, whose spokesman until his death in 1822 was Chief Justice Spencer Roane of the Virginia Supreme Court of Appeals. So able a jurist and so strong a Democratic-Republican was Roane that Jefferson had planned on his accession to the Presidency to name Roane Chief Justice of the United States. However, John Adams' "midnight appointment" of John Marshall in 1801 forestalled it and increased bitterness which existed between Jefferson and Marshall.

On the western Virginia frontier settlers lived simply amid threat of Indian attack. *Thomas L. Williams*

John Taylor of Caroline and William Branch Giles were political independents in the confused politics of nineteenth century Virginia. Each served in the Senate. *The Valentine Museum, Richmond*

Besides the mercurial Roane, the Richmond Junto included at times a half-dozen other moderates who sought to reconcile national and state powers in Virginia. Foremost was Thomas Ritchie, a cousin of Roane's and editor of the Richmond newspaper the *Enquirer*, which became the unofficial journal of the Jeffersonians and their successors in Virginia. Others were Congressman Andrew Stevenson of Albemarle County, who became Speaker of the House of Representatives from 1827 to 1834; Senator William Cabell Rives of Nelson County; Senator Benjamin Watkins Leigh of Amelia County; and Dr. John Brockenbrough of Richmond, a physician and president of the Bank of Virginia.

At the other end of the spectrum, and directly opposed to the policies of John Randolph and John Taylor, were Marshall's Federalists and their New Whig successors. From 1797 to the Civil War, their spasmodic existence gave Virginia organized political competition for the first time. The chief newspaper of the anti-Democrats in Virginia was the *Constitutional Whig*, published in Richmond by John Hampden Pleasants. Like Thomas Ritchie's *Enquirer*, it was a force in creating party spirit throughout the states which followed Virginia's lead.

However, the chief source of nationalist sentiment in Virginia was Chief Justice Marshall. In his thirty-four years on the Court he so interpreted the many vague Constitutional provisions which had been necessitated by compromise between the provinces in Philadelphia in 1787 that he strengthened the power of the national government for the years to come. His simple and clear opinions created a national power that more than offset the opposing force of the Jeffersonians' individual and states' rights. The Virginia General Assembly expressed concern that the Marshall court had created a "centripetal force" which threatened to destroy the "centrifugal force" of the states.

The Virginia Supreme Court of Appeals fought Marshall step by step during Roane's lifetime. When Marshall, in the case of McCulloch versus Maryland in 1819, denied a

Among leaders of the moderate Jeffersonians in nineteenth century Virginia were William Cabell Rives, Benjamin Watkins Leigh, and Andrew Stevenson, who became Speaker of the House of Representatives and Minister to France. *Virginia State Library. The Valentine Museum, Richmond*

State had power to tax notes of a federal agency on grounds that "the power to tax involves the power to destroy," Virginia Jeffersonians were furious. And when the U.S. Supreme Court later rejected Virginia Court decisions on grounds of error, Roane and each of his associates delivered a separate opinion refusing to re-examine the cases. Roane even wrote anonymous letters of condemnation to the *Richmond Enquirer* and the *Washington Gazette*.

Chief Justice Marshall, a little more restrained, suggested to another Supreme Court justice that he reply in the Federalist press.

"Our opinion in the Bank case has aroused the sleeping spirit of Virginia," he observed, "if, indeed, it ever sleeps." Nevertheless, Marshall persisted in his effort to strengthen the union against threat of dismemberment. Jefferson, on the other hand, was equally convinced that Marshall's interpretation of the Constitution violated the intent of its framers and created a central power which threatened the union.

This issue was debated on many levels and over many cases from the time Jefferson and Marshall took office in 1801 until well after their deaths. Indeed, it continues to this day.

10   Disillusion, Division, and Civil War

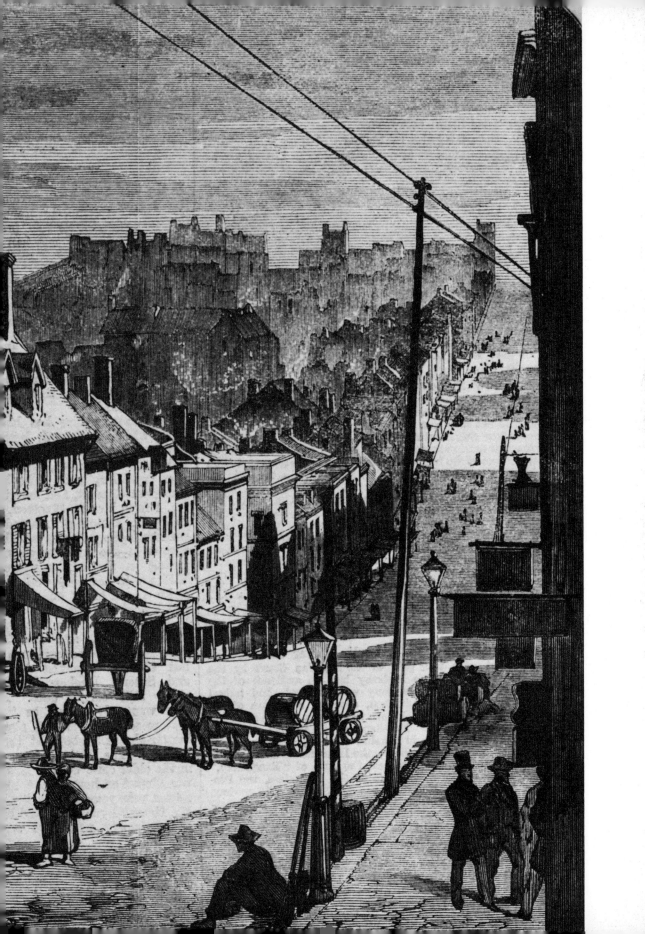

VIRGINIA FACES MOMENTOUS DECISIONS: *Internal strife, which had be-*
deviled the colonists of Jamestown, brings anxious hours to Virginia's
statesmen. Jefferson's hopes for the peaceful eradication of slavery had
not been realized. In the eastern counties the plantation owners hold on
to their economic interest in slave labor; in the west the small farmers
agitate for economic reforms. The Civil War reduces the area and wealth
of the Old Dominion.

10

Disillusion, Division, and Civil War

The bell which tolled Jefferson's death at Monticello on July 4, 1826, tolled the end of an era in America. It had been a period of difficult adjustment between state and federal powers. The idealism with which Washington had taken office in 1789 had been riddled by economic and political conflict. Then, in 1820, came the debate over the admission of Missouri to the Union. All earlier issues were dwarfed by the furor created by Congress' prohibition of slavery in the Louisiana Purchase north of a line at 36° 30′ N. Lat.

From his Charlottesville mountaintop, Jefferson saw the threat to the South posed by this new assertion of national power. "This momentous question, like a fire bell in the night, awakened and filled me with terror," the old man wrote. "I considered it at once as the knell of the Union. . . . A geographical line, coinciding with a marked principle, moral and political, once conceived and held up to the angry passions of men, will never be obliterated; and every new irritation will mark it deeper and deeper."

Like most Virginia leaders, Jefferson deplored slavery but felt it a matter for the states to resolve. He had suggested its gradual abolition to the Virginia General Assembly of 1776. "Nothing is more certainly written in the book of fate than that these people are to be free," he had written.

Despite the warnings of Jefferson and

Jefferson retired from the Presidency in 1809 and spent his last 27 years at Monticello. He studied, wrote, and sought to avert the approaching crisis. *Virginia Chamber of Commerce*

other far-sighted Southerners, the states did not act. Too many planters were dependent on slave labor. Slaves represented property worth an average of $1000 each, and neither the Commonwealth of Virginia nor the Federal government at that time offered to share the losses that owners would face in liberating them. Even those slaves freed by enlightened masters had difficulty in finding jobs and homes. How could Virginia's million whites, most of them living on farms, absorb half a milion freed Negroes? Plans for emancipation were repeatedly proposed, and some Negroes were resettled in the new African republic of Liberia, but Virginia could not bring herself to undertake the massive surgery of total emancipation.

Within Virginia the old differences between eastern planters and western small farmers were increased by their conflicting attitudes toward the role of government in making public improvements. Western Virginia lacked turnpikes and canals, and it urged State and the Federal government to build them; the east opposed this as unconstitutional. Westerners also asked the General Assembly to encourage and even to subsidize rail service from the mountainous western counties to the ports of Tidewater Virginia; eastern delegates voted down such proposals and eventually advocated a network of canals and turnpikes as an alternative.

Despite internal problems, Virginia remained a powerful force. True, the typical Virginia statesman seemed old-fashioned after the Jacksonian Democrats took over Washington in 1829, but Virginians continued to occupy many positions of power in the expanding union.

Every administration from the inauguration of John Quincy Adams in 1825 to that

Disillusion, Division, and Civil War [179]

Farm produce from North Carolina and Virginia were brought to Norfolk by Dismal
↓ Swamp Canal steamers in the years before the Civil War. *Virginia State Library*

↑ Creation of the University of Virginia in a neo-classical setting of his design was the last act of Jefferson's life. Opened in 1824, it was the first institution of higher education in America to be created under secular influence. *Virginia State Library*

Eastern Virginians threw state support behind creation of canals to link the mountainous west with Tidewater ports. This was the James River and Kanawha Canal at Richmond. *The Valentine Museum, Richmond*

Henry Clay, left, a native of Virginia, was Secretary of State in John Quincy Adams' administration and James Barbour was Secretary of War. *Clay from The Valentine Museum, Richmond. Barbour from Virginia State Library*

of Abraham Lincoln in 1861 contained Virginians or Virginia-born men. James Barbour of Orange County was Secretary of War in the younger Adams' cabinet, while Henry Clay, born at "The Slashes" in Hanover County, was Secretary of State. William Taylor Barry, a native of Lunenburg County who had moved to Kentucky, was Postmaster General under Jackson. Secretary of State under Jackson and his successor, President Martin Van Buren, was John Forsyth, a Georgian who had been born at Fredericksburg.

Elected President in 1841 was William Henry Harrison, who had migrated like so many other Virginians to the western frontier when it was the Northwest Territory. Born at Berkeley Plantation, in Charles City County, Harrison moved early in life to the Ohio Territory, where he won a famous victory over the Indians at Tippecanoe in 1811. His Vice President was John Tyler, born on another Charles City estate and a

former Governor and son of a Governor. He succeeded Harrison as President upon the latter's death a month after his inauguration.

They were the fifth and sixth Virginia-born Presidents in the first fifty years of the republic.

A promising Virginia statesman who lived too briefly in this difficult time was Abel Parker Upshur, of Virginia's Eastern Shore. After serving President Tyler as Secretary of the Navy, he became Secretary of State. Both Upshur and his successor in the Navy post, Thomas Walker Gilmer, of Albemarle, were killed in 1844 in an explosion aboard the USS Princeton. Tyler's third appointee to the Navy secretariat was John Young Mason of Greensville County. Tyler chose as his Secretary of the Treasury George Mortimer Bibb, born in Prince Edward County and removed to Kentucky.

William Ballard Preston of Montgomery County served President Zachary Taylor as

Elected President and Vice President in 1841 were William Henry Harrison and John Tyler, both born in Charles City County. Tyler (left) succeeded Harrison in office. *Thomas L. Williams*

Secretary of the Navy. President Millard Fillmore's Secretary of War was Charles Magill Conrad of Louisiana, who was a native of Winchester, while his Secretary of the Interior was Alexander Hugh Holmes Stuart of Staunton. John Buchanan Floyd of Washington County, a former Governor and son of a Governor, was Secretary of War under Buchanan, while Aaron Venable Brown, a Tennesseean who had been born in Brunswick County, was Buchanan's Postmaster-General. Even Lincoln had a Virginia-born Attorney General in Edward Bates, a native of Goochland County and a resident of Missouri.

In the realm of territorial expansion, Vir-

Prominent Virginians in the period of sectional bitterness were, left to right, Secretaries Abel Parker Upshur and Thomas Walker Gilmer of Tyler's administration, and John Buchanan Floyd, of Buchanan's cabinet. *Virginia State Library*

Early territorial governors from Virginia were, left to right, William Charles Claiborne in Mississippi and Louisiana, William Pope DuVal in Florida, and Stevens Thomson Mason in Michigan. *Virginia State Library*

General Winfield Scott began his long military career in the War of 1812. After commanding one of the two American armies in the War with Mexico, he became Chief of Staff of the United States Army before the Civil War. *The Valentine Museum, Richmond*

ginia was also active as the century rolled on. As a reward for their services in the exploration of the West, Jefferson named Meriwether Lewis governor of the Louisiana territory in 1807 and Madison named William Clark governor of Missouri Territory in 1815. Both were Albemarle County neighbors of Jefferson's; Clark was a native of Caroline County and was the younger brother of General George Rogers Clark. William Charles Coles Claiborne of Sussex became governor of the Mississippi Territory in 1801 and of Louisiana in 1812. The first territorial governor of Florida in 1822 was William Pope DuVal, of Richmond. Nineteen-year-old Stevens Thomson Mason, of Loudoun County, was appointed by President Jackson as governor of Michigan Territory in 1831 and was its first elected governor after Michigan gained statehood in 1836. When Texas was annexed to the Union in the administration of Tyler, its first governor was General Sam Houston, born in Rockbridge County.

For almost a third of the nineteenth century, two of the seven justices of the United States Supreme Court were Virginians. Bushrod Washington, a nephew of the first President, was appointed in 1798 and served until 1829, most of this time with Chief Justice Marshall presiding. After Marshall's death in 1835, President Jackson appointed to the court Philip Pendleton Barbour of Orange County, brother of James Barbour. On Barbour's death President Van Buren named Peter Vivian Daniel of Stafford County, the last appointee from Virginia ever to serve thereon.

Barbour had previously been Speaker of the House of Representatives, in which role three other Virginians closely followed him: Andrew Stevenson of Albemarle County in 1827-34; Robert Mercer Taliaferro Hunter of Essex County in 1838-41; and John Winston Jones of Amelia County in 1843-45.

The tradition of the citizen-soldier had been part of Virginia since Governor Sir William Berkeley called up the militia in 1676 to defend the capital at Jamestown against Nathaniel Bacon. In the nineteenth century, plantation-trained Virginians were still said to have "the habit of command." In battles with the British along the Canadian frontier in the War of 1812, William Henry Harrison followed up his Tippecanoe victory of 1811, and a young graduate of William and Mary, Winfield Scott of Petersburg, began the long career which

Fresh from victory in the Mexican War, Zachary Taylor was elected to the Presidency in 1848. He was the seventh Virginia-born President in 60 years. *Thomas L. Williams*

was to see him as Chief of Staff of the United States Army when the Civil War began.

Scott and another Virginian, Zachary Taylor of Orange, led the two American armies in the Mexican War over possession of Texas in 1846. In contrast to the punctilio of "Old Fuss and Feathers" Scott, Taylor had a simple fearlessness which won him the nickname "Old Rough and Ready" and catapulted him into the White House in 1848. He was the seventh Virginia-born President in sixty years.

As in each earlier war, American forces in the war with Mexico included many Virginia men. Notable for their service there were three officers recently from the new United States Military Academy: Thomas J. Jackson of Clarksburg, now West Virginia; Joseph E. Johnston of Prince Edward County; and Robert E. Lee of Westmoreland County, son of "Lighthorse Harry" Lee of the Revolution.

As the century progressed, the gulf between east and west Virginia widened. The growing possibility that the westerners might try to separate themselves from troubled Virginia led to another State Constitutional Convention in 1850 and 1851. Concerned for the future, the east at last proved willing to rewrite the law to eliminate surviving features of colonial rule, which were so bitterly resented outside the ruling eastern oligarchy. By majority vote the Convention granted the vote to all white males without restriction and permitted election by the populace of the Governor and Virginia's two United States senators. More importantly, it reapportioned seats in the General Assembly to give western counties a majority in the House of Delegates.

For the first time in Virginia's 245 years,

a resident from west of the Virginia mountains was elected Governor in 1852. He was Joseph Johnson of Harrison County, now in West Virginia.

These reforms and a revival of prosperity in the 1850s gave Virginians new hope. However, the issue of slavery had grown too violent for sober statesmanship. In 1859 Kansas abolitionist John Brown led an attack on Harpers Ferry in northwestern Virginia and seized the Federal arsenal there, planning to lead an insurrection of slaves against their masters. The revolt was put down by Virginia militia, reinforced by United States Marines under Lieut. Colonel Robert E. Lee of the Second U.S. Cavalry, but it embittered sectional feeling.

The breaking point came in 1860 when national parties split on the slavery issue. The Democrats, whom Jefferson had first organized and Andrew Jackson had revivified, broke in two and nominated both Northern and Southern candidates. A third party, advocating intersectional unity, nominated John Bell of Tennessee for President and received the majority of Virginia's vote. The fourth, and victorious, party was a coalition of Northern and Western Aboli-

Three Virginians who were conspicuous in the War with Mexico were, Thomas J. Jackson, later known as "Stonewall"; Robert E. Lee, son of "Light Horse Harry," and Joseph E. Johnston, lower left. *Virginia State Library*

tionists and others who took the Jeffersonians' old party name, Republican. Upon the Republicans' election of Abraham Lincoln, South Carolina immediately seceded, and six other Southern states followed. They formed the Confederate States of America and established a capital in Montgomery, Alabama.

Virginia's efforts to mediate and preserve the union seemed hopelessly at an end. The alternatives were to remain with the nation or to join the secessionists. The nationalist spirit of George Washington and John Marshall cried out to her to stay, while the states' rights policies of Thomas Jefferson and James Madison seemed to point to secession. Yet how could Virginia, the faithful advocate of independence and nationhood, consider renouncing the nation

which she had helped create? To former Governor James McDowell of Lexington, the choice amounted to "a question of self-interest on the one hand and self-preservation on the other."

The General Assembly called a convention in Richmond in February, 1861, in an effort to avert disunion. "Surely," Governor John Letcher told its members, "no people have been blessed as we have been, and it is melancholy to think that all is now about to be sacrificed on the altar of passion. If the judgments of men were consulted . . . the Union would yet be saved from overthrow."

Desperately, the convention invited states to send delegates to a conference in Washington to adjust their differences. Ex-President Tyler, now 70, came out of retirement

In the midcentury division over slavery and secession, western Virginians took a larger role in Virginia's leadership. James McDowell of Rockbridge County (left) was Virginia's Governor from 1843 to 1846, and John Letcher of Lexington was "War Governor" from 1860 to 1864.

to carry Virginia's request to Lincoln, while Judge John Robertson of Petersburg hurried to South Carolina to avert Confederate provocation. Predictably, Virginia's Peace Convention accomplished nothing, and Congress adjourned without seriously considering its proposals. Tyler had been a moderating influence, but he now concluded that secession was Virginia's only honorable course.

When Confederate batteries in Charleston, South Carolina, opened fire on Federal forces in Fort Sumter on April 12, 1861, Lincoln called for troops from all states to put down the insurgents. Governor Letcher refused, and on April 17 the Virginia legislative convention in Richmond voted to secede. Voters ratified an ordinance of secession by more than six to one, the pro-Union votes coming chiefly from western counties. Virginia joined the Confederacy, and Richmond became its capital.

At noon on April 23 the convention commissioned Colonel Robert E. Lee, lately resigned from the United States Army, as commander of Virginia's forces. The Virginia Capitol was crowded with onlookers as Lee mounted the portico that Jefferson had designed, on his way to take the oath of office. The white temple that overlooked the James held for him many reminders of happier years when Virginia had led the colonies toward union. Passing beneath the Rotunda on his way to the convention's chamber, Lee gazed up at the likeness of his ideal, the great nationalist George Washington, serene in marble.

Entering the hall of the House of Delegates, where the convention was assembled, the erect soldier in mufti stood where his father had opposed the adoption of the Virginia Resolutions of 1798 against the Alien and Sedition Acts; no man could have been a more ardent advocate of union than

"Lighthorse Harry" Lee had been. Indeed, many of the noblest hopes of the new nation had been voiced in this Capitol. Now Virginia was leaving that union.

With little trace of emotion the solemn Lee accepted responsibility to defend Virginia against invasion by the United States. It was rumored that Winfield Scott had offered him command of the Union forces — a command which in other circumstances would have been a capstone to the career of a professional soldier such as Lee. However, in the conflict of loyalties within him, it seemed to Lee, as to most Virginians, that his first duty was to the Old Dominion. Patrick Henry had said it many years before: "They were Virginians first."

Responding to the convention's president, Lee embarked Virginia on its desperate course. "Trusting in almighty God, an approving conscience, and the aid of my fellow-citizens," he said, "I devote myself to the service of my native State, in whose behalf alone will I ever again draw my sword."

Lee spoke for most Virginians, but not all. There were important exceptions. The majority of settlers west of the Allegheny Mountains never had given first allegiance to Virginia, but to the nation. They had little in common with the eastern Virginian aristocracy, which had developed in colonial days and had resisted western encroachment on its power. Opposing Virginia's

Claims west of the Mississippi River Relinquished by Britain, 1753

Northwest Territory

West Virginia

Kentucky

Virginia

The secession of West Virginia in 1863 reduced Virginia to its present size. The empire she had possessed when she entered the union was hers no more. Map by William Gravitt, adapted from *A Hornbook of Virginia History*

withdrawal from the Union, delegates from the western counties gathered in Wheeling in 1862 and secretly initiated their own secession. The state of West Virginia, constituting approximately a third of the Old Dominion, was torn from Virginia in the midst of war and accepted in the Union in 1863.

With this division the great Virginia empire was no more. From an expanse of 313,279 square miles before she entered the Union, the Old Dominion was now reduced to 40,815 square miles and a few more than 1,000,000 people. More importantly, many of the qualities that had made her the leader among the colonies now placed her out of the mainstream in a competitive and equalitarian age. She no longer had the physical size, the wealth, or the population to hold front rank in a democracy of numbers. The eighteenth century suddenly seemed far away. The English ideas that Virginia had first planted in America were giving way to a new Yankee age.

Still and all, Virginia's qualities stemmed from her innermost character. She could not change those qualities if she would. She did not apologize for them, even though she stood to lose all that she valued. They were the accretion of generations lived in accordance with a proud creed; lived in the same homes, on the same acres, with the same ideals of man's duty to himself, his family, his land, his God. Whatever might come, there would be the consolation of knowing she did what she thought she must, without counting the cost.

In this spirit Virginia plunged into the holocaust of the Civil War, trusting that right would prevail.

Epilogue

Epilogue

More than 350 years have elapsed since English settlement of the New World began at Jamestown, yet Virginia preserves much that its first settlers brought with them.

This continuity is more than habit. It grows from a strong British legacy, which has created cultural unity among the people of Virginia and other areas of the South, as well as of parts of New England. Because of this persistence, Virginia in some respects seems provincial in spirit. Yet it is a defect which has its virtues. Many simple values of the unsophisticated past — personal independence, a high sense of honor, close family ties, gentleness of manner — these have not succumbed in most sections of Virginia to the moral relativism of the age.

Another force for continuity is the preponderance of rural strength until recently in Virginia life. Now, however, the industrial boom which followed World War II has given urban Virginia more votes than the counties. A more marked conflict between urban and rural interests is beginning to appear, lead-

The tower of the church begun in 1639 is the oldest surviving structure of Jamestown's settlement. The first Virginia Assembly of 1619 is believed to have met on this site. *Virginia Chamber of Commerce*

ing to wider competition for office. Virginia's traditional preference for government by consensus to government by party may be giving way to a genuine two-party system. Yet the spirit of Sir Edwin Sandys' Country Party remains dominant after 350 years.

A traditionalism that respects age and seniority also persists. In recent years, as in the days of the Council of State, the ballot in Virginia has been restricted to the well-educated, eliminating most Negroes as voters. However, the improved education of Negroes and the recent elimination by Congressional action of the poll tax prerequisite in Federal elections is changing this, too.

As has been pointed out, Virginia has experienced relatively little organized party competition for office in her history. The Democratic party of Jefferson and Andrew Jackson has been predominant since Virginians reasserted their political will following Reconstruction. Not since 1882 has the Old Dominion elected a Republican governor, despite her support of the Republican Presidential candidate — in each case more conservative than the Democratic nominee — in the national elections of 1952, 1956, and 1960. Now there are indications that the Virginia electorate may divide more in keeping with party lines in other states as industry grows in Virginia.

Preference for local government also persists. In the continuing adjustment between states and nation, the majority of Virginians believe their best interests to be served by maintaining a high degree of local control. Virginians in Congress continue to exercise leadership in defense of states' rights. Though most of them have been Democrats, they have largely opposed the extension of federal power proposed by every President since Franklin D. Roosevelt.

Industrialization has relieved Virginia of much of her earlier dependence on agriculture. Diversification of the state's economy which was interrupted by the Civil War has progressed rapidly in recent years. Today only a few remote rural counties, chiefly in the tobacco country south of the James River, remain unaffected by twentieth century industry. Country life steadily gives ground to interstate freeways and suburbs. Similarly, the paternalism which dulled the sting of slavery for centuries in Virginia is being superseded by industrial employment and by Federal guarantees of jobs and rights.

Although her long dependence on agriculture cost Virginia much money, it prevented the development of extremes of wealth and poverty as well as conflicts between capital and labor which accompanied nineteenth century industrialization in northern states. In this respect, agriculture's long reign has made for social cohesiveness. The Virginia gentleman farmer, dirt farmer, and tenant farmer share a common hardship that has contributed to mutual understanding, whatever their differences of race or income might be. Over the years, as John Marshall observed in 1829, no people have enjoyed more peaceable dealings with each other than Virginia's.

Beneath this complex of attitudes one finds many characteristics which link the present with the past. The similarity goes deeper than names, speech, or social habits. It is founded on a sense of values that is idealistic and fundamentalist Christian, on a morality simple and Calvinistic. The moral relativism of twentieth century America has made little headway against the Old Testament conception of right and wrong, which most Virginians accept from the past. The pragmatism of current national politics seems to them simply a subtle dishonesty.

The unconscious model of Virginians since Governor Berkeley's day has been the English country squire, an upright and hearty citizen who served his parish as vestryman, who promoted the welfare of his servants and tenants, and who answered the call to arms or to public office when he heard it. Such a life, lived amid family and rural pleasures, was the ideal of Robert Carter of Nomini Hall, of George Mason of Gunston Hall, and of George Washington. It is an ideal that has motivated more than fifteen generations of Virginians since 1607.

This conception places a greater value on the freedom of rural life than on the comfort of the city. "In the breast of every Virginian," wrote that arch-Virginian, John Randolph, "if he was not so fortunate as to inherit, or expect to inherit, such a plantation, was the resolve to realize his ideal of perfect felicity by sooner or later buying one and spending the remainder of his days on it in the enjoyment of the rural pleasures, which are among the few human pleasures that leave no bitter taste in the mouth." In an age of exploding population many Virginians cherish a serene isolation.

To early Virginians, "simplicity" was the first requisite of a public man, being the opposite of "cleverness," or self-interest. The Virginia-born Presidents exemplified this sense of honor in office. To a remarkable degree, it also has been characteristic of Virginians who have held office in all periods. The ideal of public service for the sake of its honor rather than salary or fringe benefits is a survival of Jefferson's age.

The sense of the past created by Virginia's wealth of history contributes to the social conservatism of its people. That which has been dignified by age and honorable usage is accorded a respect in the Old Dominion not usual elsewhere in breathlessly ongoing America. Old houses, roads, and customs are cherished, regardless of fickle fashion. The antiquarian and genealogist flourish. Restorations of historic homes, churches, and public buildings abound in

Virginia's laws were made in the Christopher Wren Building of the College of William and Mary from 1700 to 1705 and again from 1747 to 1753, after the first Williamsburg Capitol burned. It is the oldest academic building in the United States. *Colonial Williamsburg*

Tidewater Virginia as nowhere else in the United States. This zeal to preserve has given birth to a wealth of historical societies and has saved many remnants of colonial America which otherwise would have been flattened.

Tidewater Virginia also practices a mild Shintoism, as Dr. Douglas Southall Freeman observed. Nowhere are family arms displayed more proudly. Nowhere are family relationships more carefully kept alive or "cousins" more faithfully remembered. Such organizations as the Association for the Preservation of Virginia Antiquities, the Virginia Historical Society, and the Garden Club of Virginia attest this interest. The vigor of Virginia's preservation effort has been widely recognized and emulated.

Washington and Lee University at Lexington is the oldest institution of learning planted by the Scotch-Irish in the Virginia Valley. It began as John Brown's Academy in 1749 and grew after Washington gave it $50,000 worth of canal stock. *Virginia Chamber of Commerce*

FACING PAGE: Virginia's first Capitol in Williamsburg was put to use in 1704. It burned in 1747 and was replaced by a similar structure. This is a reconstruction of the first building, with the Governor's Council chamber at left and the Burgesses' chamber at right. *Colonial Williamsburg*

Virginians remain in large degree puritans and fundamentalists in religion. The wave of Calvinist sobriety which swept the South in the 1820's still shows itself in opposition to public sale of alcoholic drinks and in legalized betting on horse races. In this respect Virginia has rejected the liberal attitudes of its first settlers. Because of the reaction to Anglicanism during the American Revolution and afterward, the Cavalier State has ceased to be a stronghold of the blooded horse or the frosted julep. Blue laws until recently inhibited Sunday recreation and commerce, but they are rapidly disappearing.

Allied to Virginians' love for land and exploration is their military tradition. It flourishes today as before, nurtured by memories of great leaders and bloody victories in every war in the nation's history. The all-but-unique Virginia Military Institute, founded in 1839, and a host of military academies continue to kindle the spirit of valor. In war and peace Virginia has a high rate of enlistment in the armed forces. Five of the twenty-three commandants of the U. S. Marine Corps since its beginning have been natives of the Old Dominion.

Dominant as Virginia's English heritage is, one must not overlook other major influences. The imprint of the Negro is clearly on Virginia's speech, folklore, music, humor, and cuisine. The State has been greatly enriched by its legacies from the Germanic settlements in the Valley of Virginia and from the Huguenots of southern France in Powhatan and Goochland counties, along the upper James. And there are always the Scotch-Irish. The bitter colonial rivalry between these Valley settlers, known as "Cohees," and the English "Tuckahoes" of Tidewater long ago subsided. Sectionalism has waned, and the two streams flow as one.

Much as Virginia stands for today, one cannot escape thoughts of how much more she might have been but for the Civil War. In fairness, however, let us remember Virginia's long and patient efforts to serve as mediator between extremist elements in the years leading to that conflict. In the words of Vernon Louis Parrington in *The Romantic Revolution in America*, "Until the problem of slavery became acute, and leadership passed from moderate Virginians to fire-eaters from further south, the influence of Virginia at Washington was thrown on the side of republican simplicity, low taxes, and the decentralization of power. The armed clash over slavery very probably might have been averted if the spirit of the Old Dominion had prevailed."

Let us take leave of Virginia, remembering not her defeat but her triumphs. Hers was the beginning of permanent English settlement of the New World and of the growth outside the British Isles of the Anglican Church. Virginia's start was the start of the long movement of British peoples to over-

George Washington's home at Mount Vernon is a national shrine, as are the homes of Jefferson, the Lees, George Mason, and other leaders. *Virginia Chamber of Commerce*

seas dominions that resulted in the global Commonwealth of Nations. Her charters of 1606 and 1609, together with Captain Samuel Argall's subjection of the French colonies in Maine and Nova Scotia, helped secure a large section of North America for British settlement.

Later, Virginia's soldiery saved the Northwest Territory for Great Britain in the French and Indian Wars, while Virginia in the Revolution defended the same area against the British themselves and averted its annexation by Canada. For the benefit of the new United States of America, Virginia in 1784 ceded the Territory that became Ohio, Illinois, Indiana, Michigan, Wisconsin, and part of Minnesota. Eight years later she also gave up her Kentucky Territory in the interest of statehood.

Extensive as these contributions were, they were surpassed by the qualities of character and by the example of leadership which she gave to early America. "Between the older colonial America and later industrial America," wrote Parrington, "stand the ideals of the Old Dominion, more humane and generous than either, disseminating the principles of French romantic philosophy and instilling into the provincial American mind, static and stagnant in the grip of English colonialism, the ideal of democratic equalitarianism and the hope of humane progress. The nineteenth century first entered America by way of the James River."

Such was Virginia in her greatest years.

Index

G

Gama, Vasco da, 25
Garden Club of Virginia, 199
Gaspé Peninsula, 92
Gates, Thomas, 64, 89
General Assembly, Virginia, 77, 78, 92, 101, 102, 107, 120, 121, 123, 127, 129, 131, 132, 143, 147, 149, 165, 166, 171, 177, 179, 186, 187
General History of Virginia, 62
George III, of England, 110, 123
Georgia, 91, 144
Germans, in Virginia, 114, 165, 202
Gilbert, Bartholomew, 41
Gilbert, Humphrey, 27, 28, 29, 31, 32, 41
Giles, William Branch, 170, 171
Gilmer, Thomas Walker, 182, 183
Godspeed (ship), 39, 43, 46
Gosnold, Bartholomew, 41, 42, 43, 46, 49, 64
Governor's Council of State, in Virginia, 77, 78, 81, 103, 107, 166
Grasse, Comte de, 129
Great Charter of Privileges, Orders, and Laws, The, 73
Great Lakes, 91, 96, 124, 132, 159
Green Spring, Berkeley's circle at, 80, 81
Grenville, Richard, 30, 64
Griffin, Cyrus, 108, 109
Gulf of Mexico, 92, 93
Gulf of St. Lawrence, 96

H

Hamilton, Alexander, 145, 146, 148, 149
Hampden-Sydney College, 114, 160
Hampton, Virginia, 71, 107
Harpers Ferry, West Virginia, 186
Harrison, Benjamin, 123, 144, 147
Harrison, William Henry, 182, 183, 185
Harrodsburg, Kentucky, 163
Harvard College, 103, 152; founding of, 101
Harvey, John, 79
Havana, Cuba, 28
Hawkins, John, 26, 27, 31
Hawthorne, Nathaniel, 152

Henricus, Virginia, 71, 72
Henry VIII, of England, 25, 26, 60
Henry VII, of England, 25
Henry, Patrick, 107, 108, 110, 117, 121, 123, 131, 142, 146, 147, 148, 167, 170, 189
Henry the Navigator, 23
Hog Island, 64
Hojeda, Alonso de, 25
House of Burgesses, Virginia, 77, 81, 107, 108, 121, 123
House of Representatives, United States, 144, 147
Houston, Sam, 161, 185
Hudson, Henry, 92
Hudson River, 88
Huguenots, in Virginia, 111, 114, 202
Hunt, Robert, 62
Hunt, Thomas, 47
Hunter, Robert Mercer Taliaferro, 185

I

Illinois, 95, 124, 204
Indiana, 204
Indians, 58, 71, 77, 108, 163, 182; brought to London, 41; early Virginian exploring party attacked by, 47; Spanish settlers killed by, 52; Virginia massacres by, 70, 72, 75, 79
Inglis, Mungo, 110
Isabella, Queen, of Spain, 23
Italy, 24

J

Jackson, Andrew, 169, 182, 185, 186
Jackson, Thomas J., 186, 187
James I, of England, 30, 41, 42, 43, 44, 46, 58, 64, 76, 101, 120
James II, of England, 101
James Fort, 59, 63, 64, 65, 71, 73
James River, 50, 64, 65, 66, 71, 77, 87, 92, 94, 95, 101, 111, 114, 131, 162, 181, 197, 204; tobacco shipment on, 121
Jamestown, 50, 52, 58, 60, 63-66 *passim*, 71-81 *passim*, 89, 101, 102, 104, 108, 195, 196; arrival of settlers at (1607), 49, 52; brick house